Modern Middle East Nations

AND THEIR STRATEGIC PLACE IN THE WORLD

ISRAEL

33°E 34°E 35°E 36°E 37°E

LEBANON

SYRIA

Haifa

Tiberias

*Sea of
Galilee*

*Sea
Ga*

Nazareth

33°N

Mediterranean

**West
Bank**

Jordan River

Sea

Tel Aviv-Yafo

32°N

Jerusalem ✪

*Dead
Sea*

**Gaza
Strip**

Gaza

JORDAN

Beersheba

31°N

ISRAEL

N

W   E

S

EGYPT

NEGEV

Occupied
by Israel
since 1967

30°N

Elat

0   20   40 Miles

0   20   40 Kilometers

Conic Projection

Gulf of Aqaba

**SAUDI
ARABIA**

29°N

Modern Middle East Nations

AND THEIR STRATEGIC PLACE IN THE WORLD

ISRAEL

ADAM GARFINKLE

MASON CREST PUBLISHERS
PHILADELPHIA

Produced by OTTN Publishing, Stockton, New Jersey

Mason Crest Publishers
370 Reed Road
Broomall, PA 19008
www.masoncrest.com

First printing

1 3 5 7 9 8 6 4 2

Library of Congress Cataloging-in-Publication Data

Garfinkle, Adam M., 1951-
  Israel / Adam Garfinkle.
      p. cm. — (Modern Middle East nations and their strategic place in the world)
  Summary: Discusses the geography, history, economy, government,
  religion, people, foreign relations, and communities of Israel.
  Includes bibliographical references and index.
    ISBN 1-59084-552-8
  1. Israel—Juvenile literature. [1. Israel.] I. Title. II. Series.

  DS126.5.G356 2003 956.94—dc21

                                    2003000901

Modern Middle East Nations
AND THEIR STRATEGIC PLACE IN THE WORLD

TABLE OF CONTENTS

Modern Middle East Nations
AND THEIR STRATEGIC PLACE IN THE WORLD

Dr. Harvey Sicherman, president and director of the Foreign Policy Research Institute, is the author of such books as *America the Vulnerable: Our Military Problems and How to Fix Them* (2002) and *Palestinian Autonomy, Self-Government and Peace* (1993).

Introduction

by Dr. Harvey Sicherman

Situated as it is between Africa, Europe, and the Far East, the Middle East has played a unique role in world history. Often described as the birthplace of religions (notably Judaism, Christianity, and Islam) and the cradle of civilizations (Egypt, Mesopotamia, Persia), this region and its peoples have given humanity some of its most precious possessions. At the same time, the Middle East has had more than its share of conflicts. The area is strewn with the ruins of fortifications and the cemeteries of combatants, not to speak of modern arsenals for war.

Today, more than ever, Americans are aware that events in the Middle East can affect our security and prosperity. The United States has a considerable military, political, and economic presence throughout much of the region. Developments there regularly find their way onto the front pages of our newspapers and the screens of our television sets.

Still, it is fair to say that most Middle Eastern countries remain a mystery, their cultures and religions barely known, their peoples and politics confusing and strange. The purpose of this book series is to change that, to educate the reader in the basic facts about the 23 states and many peoples that make up the region. (For our purpose, the Middle East also includes the North African states linked by ethnicity, language, and religion to the Arabs, as well as Somalia and Mauritania, which are African but share the Muslim religion and are members of the Arab League.) A notable feature of the series is the integration of geography, demography, and history; economics and politics; culture and religion. The careful student will learn much that he or she needs to know about ever so important lands.

A few general observations are in order as an introduction to the subject matter.

The first has to do with history and politics. The modern Middle East is full of ancient sites and peoples who trace their lineage and literature to antiquity. Many commentators also attribute the Middle East's political conflicts to grievances and rivalries from the distant past. While history is often invoked, the truth is that the modern Middle East political system dates only from the 1920s and was largely created by the British and the French, the victors of World War I. Such states as Algeria, Iraq, Israel, Jordan, Kuwait, Saudi Arabia, Syria, Turkey, and the United Arab Emirates did not exist before 1914—they became independent between 1920 and 1971. Others, such as Egypt and Iran, were dominated by outside powers until well after World War II. Before 1914, most of the region's states were either controlled by the Turkish-run Ottoman Empire or owed allegiance to the Ottoman sultan. (The sultan was also the caliph or highest religious authority in Islam, in the line of the prophet Muhammad's successors, according to the beliefs of the majority of Muslims known as the Sunni.) It was this imperial Muslim system that was ended by the largely British military victory over the Ottomans in World War I. Few of the leaders who emerged in the wake of this event were happy with the territories they were assigned or the borders, which were often drawn by Europeans. Yet, the system has endured despite many efforts to change it.

The second observation has to do with economics, demography, and natural resources. The Middle Eastern peoples live in a region of often dramatic geographical contrasts: vast parched deserts and high mountains, some with year-round snow; stone-hard volcanic rifts and lush semi-tropical valleys; extremely dry and extremely wet conditions, sometimes separated by only a few miles; large permanent rivers and wadis, riverbeds dry as a bone until winter rains send torrents of flood from the mountains to the sea. In ancient times, a very skilled agriculture made the Middle East the breadbasket of the Roman Empire, and its trade carried luxury fabrics, foods, and spices both East and West.

Most recently, however, the Middle East has become more known for a single commodity—oil, which is unevenly distributed and largely concentrated in the Persian Gulf and Arabian Peninsula (although large pockets are also to be found in Algeria, Libya, and other sites). There are also new, potentially lucrative offshore gas fields in the Eastern Mediterranean.

This uneven distribution of wealth has been compounded by demographics. Birth rates are very high, but the countries with the most oil are often lightly populated. Over the last decade, Middle East populations under the age of 20 have grown enormously. How will these young people be educated? Where will they work? The failure of most governments in the region to give their people skills and jobs (with notable exceptions such as Israel) has also contributed to large out-migrations. Many have gone to Europe; many others work in other Middle Eastern countries, supporting their families from afar.

Another unsettling situation is the heavy pressure both people and industry have put on vital resources. Chronic water shortages plague the region. Air quality, public sanitation, and health services in the big cities are also seriously overburdened. There are solutions to these problems, but they require a cooperative approach that is sorely lacking.

A third important observation is the role of religion in the Middle East. Americans, who take separation of church and state for granted, should know that most countries in the region either proclaim their countries to be Muslim or allow a very large role for that religion in public life. Among those with predominantly Muslim populations, Turkey alone describes itself as secular and prohibits avowedly religious parties in the political system. Lebanon was a Christian-dominated state, and Israel continues to be a Jewish state. While both strongly emphasize secular politics, religion plays an enormous role in culture, daily life, and legislation. It is also important to recall that Islamic law (*Sharia*) permits people to practice Judaism and Christianity in Muslim states but only as *Dhimmi*, protected but very second-class citizens.

Fourth, the American student of the modern Middle East will be impressed by the varieties of one-man, centralized rule, very unlike the workings of Western democracies. There are monarchies, some with traditional methods of consultation for tribal elders and even ordinary citizens, in Saudi Arabia and many Gulf States; kings with limited but still important parliaments (such as in Jordan and

Morocco); and military and civilian dictatorships, some (such as Syria) even operating on the hereditary principle (Hafez al Assad's son Bashar succeeded him). Turkey is a practicing democracy, although a special role is given to the military that limits what any government can do. Israel operates the freest democracy, albeit constricted by emergency regulations (such as military censorship) due to the Arab-Israeli conflict.

In conclusion, the MODERN MIDDLE EAST NATIONS series will engage imagination and interest simply because it covers an area of such great importance to the United States. Americans may be relative latecomers to the affairs of this region, but our involvement there will endure. We at the Foreign Policy Research Institute hope that these books will kindle a lifelong interest in the fascinating and significant Middle East.

A Jewish cemetery on the Mount of Olives overlooks the skyline of Jerusalem. A prominent feature is the Dome of the Rock. Jerusalem is considered a holy place by the followers of three of the world's great monotheistic religions—Judaism, Christianity, and Islam.

Place in the World

Israel is the most unusual country in the Middle East, and possibly in the whole world. It is easy to understand some of the basic reasons for this.

First, every other country in the Middle East is defined culturally by its Islamic civilization (even if non-Muslim minorities also live within these countries' borders), but Israel is defined by its Jewish civilization (though it, similarly, is home to non-Jewish minorities). Israel is the only majority-Jewish country in the world.

A NATION BOTH ANCIENT AND MODERN

Second, while Israel is a relatively new country, established as an independent state in 1948, Jewish civilization flourished on the land that is now Israel thousands of years ago. The ancient kingdoms of Israel, led by such men as can be read about in the Bible—Saul, David, Solomon, and others—are known historically as the First and Second Jewish Commonwealths. Together, they ruled what is today Israel as an independent political entity for more than 1,600 years (the United States, by contrast, is less than 250 years old). But Jewish national independence in the Middle East was extinguished through conquest by the Roman Empire, and most Jews were exiled from their homeland around A.D. 135. Some Jews came back over the centuries, and certain places in Israel—Jerusalem, Tiberias, Safad, and Hebron, for example— always maintained Jewish communities. But significant numbers of Jews did not begin to return to the country, by then known as Palestine, until the end of the 19th century. No other people in history has ever managed to maintain its identity over such a long period without being able to live together, and no other people has been able to reestablish its national independence after so long a break.

Relatedly, the main language in Israel is Hebrew, and Israel is the only country in the world where the majority speaks Hebrew. While the language is not identical to the ancient Hebrew of the Bible, it is close enough so that all educated Jewish Israelis can easily read their ancient literature—far more readily, for example, than native English-speakers can read *Beowulf*, or the works of Chaucer or even Shakespeare. There are no other such examples in the world today; modern Greeks cannot readily read ancient Greek, modern Iranians cannot easily decipher ancient Persian texts, and so on.

Most Israelis also speak some English, which they learn in school and are exposed to through cable television, movies, and other forms of entertainment. Israelis in professional walks of life almost all speak English fluently. Israeli Arabs speak Arabic as their first language, but most know Hebrew. Many Jewish Israelis, whose families came from the Middle Eastern countries, also speak and understand Arabic.

A SMALL COUNTRY WITH BIG INFLUENCE

Third, Israel is one of the smallest countries in the world—only about the size of New Jersey. And not very many people live there: by mid-2002 Israel's estimated population was just over 6 million; more people live in New York City alone. About 80 percent of Israel's people, some 4.8 million, are Jewish. (Most of the rest are Arabs, the majority of them Muslims, but Israel also has a significant Christian Arab population.)

Israel's 6 million citizens constitute less than one-tenth of one percent of the world's total population of more than 6 billion. And yet, in some ways, Israel figures pretty large. It is in the news a lot, for reasons we will examine later. But in many respects Israel is also powerful beyond its size. It is a relatively wealthy country: in 2001,

The people of Israel are a culturally diverse lot, reflecting the fact that Israelis may have come from any number of countries throughout the world.

according to the World Bank, it boasted the world's 35th-largest economy, ahead of a host of more populous nations. And Israel's 2001 ***gross domestic product*** (GDP) per capita—a measure of each citizen's average share of the wealth generated by the country's economic activity—stood at an estimated $20,000, higher than the GDP per capita of such prosperous Western countries as Spain, New Zealand, Portugal, and Greece. Militarily, Israel is quite strong. It is acknowledged to possess nuclear weapons—one of only eight or nine such countries in the world. The achievements of its people in scientific-technical areas and in the arts and business are also way out of proportion to the small size of its population (a fact that is true, as well, for Jews as a whole relative to the world population). Per capita, Israel has more citizens who are university graduates than every other nation except the United States and the Netherlands. It has the highest per capita number of scientists and published scientific papers in the world. As of 2002, about 54 percent of Israelis owned personal computers; by comparison, the percentage in the United States was 42 percent.

CULTURAL DIVERSITY

Fourth, Israel is a difficult country to define culturally. Its Jewish character is central, but Jews in Israel have diverse backgrounds, reflecting the nature of their dispersion in exile for so many centuries. Most Israelis are not religious, though they recognize the centrality of religion in their becoming and remaining a single people in history; those Israelis who are religious, however, have an important influence in society and in the government. Most of the 19th- and early-20th-century immigrants back to the land were from Europe, and much of what a visitor sees in Israel today fits easily into a European (or American) mold—how most people dress, what they like to eat, how they design their buildings and their towns, for example. Other peoples in the region tend to think of Israel as largely European in character for this reason. But today the majority of Israel's citizens were neither born in, nor ever lived in, Europe. Rather, most were born in other Middle Eastern countries or in Israel, and they give the country a distinctly Middle Eastern flavor.

THE SECURITY DILEMMA

Fifth and finally for now, Israel is unusual because it is the only country in the world whose right to exist is not recognized, and is avowedly rejected, by the governments of many of its neighbors— including Syria, Iraq, Iran, Saudi Arabia, and Libya—and by significant numbers of other people around the world. Other small states such as Lichtenstein, Luxembourg, Monaco, and Andorra do exist, but no one proposes making them disappear by force. The Iraqi government and some of its people believe that Kuwait should belong to Iraq; indeed, a war was fought over that question in 1991. But outside of Iraq, virtually no one questions the right of Kuwait to exist as an independent country. Similarly, many South Koreans wish to see their country reunited with North Korea, and China believes that the island nation of Taiwan properly belongs to it. But Israel's situation is unique: its enemies' stated wish has not been to incorporate Israeli territory into their own countries but to destroy the State of Israel and its people—and on several occasions over the past five decades they have tried to accomplish that goal by force.

This fact casts very important shadows. It explains, for example, why Israel has focused to such a great extent on its military power. It explains the wars that Israel has had to fight, the attempts at making peace (some of them successful) that it has undertaken, and the dilemma it faces in dealing with Palestinian Arabs and the creation of an independent Palestinian state on Israel's borders. It also has defined the nature of Israel's relationships with countries outside the Middle East, including the United States, Russia,

China, and the European nations. The evolution of Israeli society and politics, and the relationship between Israel's Jewish majority and Arab minority, have also been much affected by this reality. So has the relationship between Jews in Israel and Jews elsewhere in the world.

Israel's security dilemma also links its circumstances to Jewish history more broadly, but exactly how is a matter of much debate. When a large percentage of the world's Jews lived in Europe, throughout much of the past two millennia, for the most part they neither wished to, nor were allowed to, assimilate into the Christian societies in which they resided. Like Gypsies and a few other minority peoples, Jews lived within Europe but apart from its mainstream society. For a variety of reasons, this condition of

Jewish children, released from a Nazi concentration camp, are on their way to Palestine in a photo taken in June 1945. Like these three Jews from eastern Europe, a large percentage of the people of Israel came to the land to escape anti-Semitism in their homelands.

physical proximity but cultural separation led some Europeans to dislike, and even hate, Jews as a group. In the 19th and 20th century, this phenomenon became known as **anti-Semitism**, and it culminated in the murder of about 6 million Jews by the Nazi regime in Germany (and some of its allies) during World War II. Most observers believe that historical anti-Semitism—which had a different and far less virulent history and nature in the Muslim world—still plays at least some role in the anti-Israel sentiments of Europeans and some other Christians; but there is a wide divergence of opinion about how significant that role is. This difference of opinion affects political analyses and diplomatic assessments today.

Of course, not everything about Israel is unusual. Just as in all other countries, the sun rises and the sun sets; the seasons change and weather is a topic of conversation. Israelis care about their families and futures, and sometimes they think about the past. They like sports (soccer, basketball, and tennis especially) and go to the movies. Children attend school (and complain about it, naturally)—and some go on to college. Israelis sometimes do exceptionally kind things and they sometimes lose their tempers. They drive cars, ride buses, have bank accounts, visit the zoo, swim at the beach, eat pizza, and walk their dogs, just like people all over the world. But the differences are there, sometimes subtly, sometimes not so subtly. For example, only recently have many Americans found out what it is like to experience terrorism on their own soil, and that reality has brought profound changes in attitudes and outlooks. Consider that Israelis have been living with terrorism, to one degree or another, for decades—longer than today's American middle school, high school, or even college students have been alive.

A vacationer, reading a tour guide on Israel, floats in the Dead Sea, the lowest place on earth. The water of the Dead Sea, believed to have healing powers, is so laden with salt that people will not sink below the surface.

The Land

Because of technological advances, people today are not as tied to the physical environment are they once were. Yet the physical environment is still important. Just as every human personality needs a physical body to carry it around, so every nation needs a place in which to exist. In the case of Jewish history, what was most notable about the Jewish people for more than 1,800 years was that they did *not* have a shared physical land on which they lived. In modern Israel, the land restored to its exiled inhabitants therefore has both symbolic as well as real significance. In this chapter we will leave aside symbolic matters, which will be elaborated elsewhere, and talk only of the physical.

In terms of physical environment, the essential facts are these: Israel is small yet ecologically very diverse, generally poor in natural resources, and situated at a crossroads of continents.

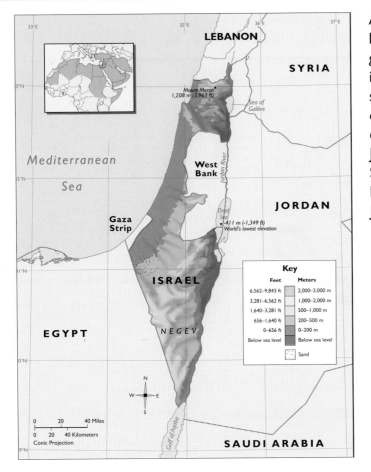

Along the coast of Israel, a low plain runs inland, gradually rising to mountains in the northern and southern parts of the country. The Negev Desert covers southern Israel. The Jordan River and the Dead Sea provide a natural boundary between Israel and Jordan.

LOCATION AND SIZE

Israel is located in the heart of the Middle East, along the eastern shores of the Mediterranean Sea (an area sometimes called the Levant). To its north is Lebanon; to the northeast, Syria; to the south, Egypt; and to the east, Jordan and the West Bank, a proposed Palestinian state whose nature and boundaries are still to be decided. In its original (pre-1967) borders, Israel comprises about 8,000 square miles (or 20,700 square kilometers). That's about the size of New Jersey.

After the so-called Six-Day War in June 1967, however, Israel occupied other territories, including Egypt's Sinai Peninsula and Syria's Golan Heights, which increased the size of the land Israel controlled to about 35,000 square miles (90,650 sq km). Sinai, a relatively large, mostly barren desert area, was returned to Egypt in the context of a peace treaty signed in March 1979. Israel still administers the Golan Heights and two other territories: the Gaza Strip and the West Bank. Together, these latter territories comprise about 2,400 square miles (6,220 sq km)—a little over 30 percent of the size of Israel before 1967—and some of these two areas are under the administration of the Palestinian Authority (since about the beginning of 1996). But none of these areas are considered by the Israeli government to be legally part of Israel, even though Israel extended Israeli law to the Golan Heights in 1981. Their status is still to be determined by negotiations between Israel and some of its neighbors. These political factors account for why different sources written at different times give different figures for the size of Israel. At any rate, what should be kept in mind is that with the exception of Lebanon, Israel is far smaller than its neighbors.

A DRY LAND

Within Israel's small area, there is considerable natural diversity. For the most part, though, Israel receives little rainfall. The entire southern half of the country is dominated by the Negev Desert. In the northern part of the desert, near the city of Beersheba, annual rainfall averages a scant 8 inches (20 centimeters); in the south, near the Red Sea port of Eilat (also spelled Elat), only about 1 inch (2.54 cm) of rain falls per year. On Israel's Mediterranean coast, average annual rainfall is higher—about 19 inches (48 cm) per year. And farther north, closer to the Lebanon border, the figure is about 24 inches (61 cm). By comparison, average annual precipitation in the Mid-Atlantic region of the United States totals about 45 inches (114 cm).

Moreover, with rare exceptions, it rains in Israel only between October and April. In the late spring and early autumn, very little rain falls; in the summer, none at all (except for very rare brief, intense showers after desert windstorms known as the *hamsin*). Few Americans have experienced a five-month period without seeing any rain, but this is normal in Israel and some neighboring countries. In addition, the rainfall patterns from year to year are erratic. Scientists have detected weather patterns in 7- and 40-year cycles, but for practical purposes the rainfall patterns mean that in some years there are winter floods, and in others there is too little water to get by on comfortably in the dry season. (During the first years of the 21st century, Israel and surrounding areas were in the midst of a very dry cycle.)

As might be expected, the rainier parts of the country are greener. Israel's northern area, called the Upper Galilee, is quite verdant, especially during the rainy season. Evergreens, deciduous trees, and many other kinds of vegetation flourish there. The Hula Valley, north of Lake Tiberias (also called the Sea of Galilee), is an agricultural region that enjoys ample freshwater. In the hillier areas of northern Israel, around Mount Carmel, near Haifa, and around the

A view of the Negev Desert, which covers the southern half of Israel. Although there is not enough rainfall in the Negev to support farming, Israelis have irrigated some parts of the desert with water from the Sea of Galilee.

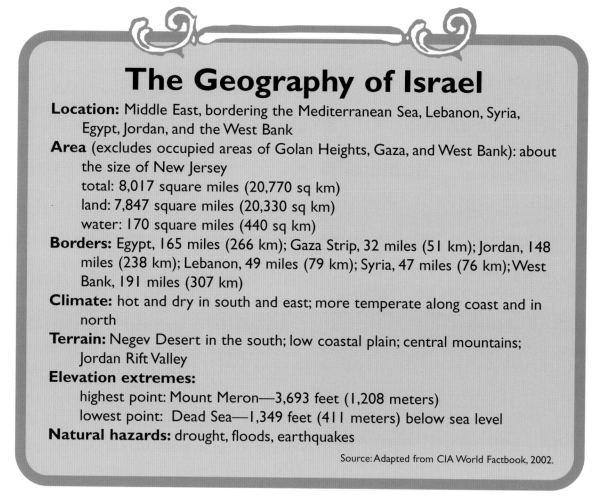

The Geography of Israel

Location: Middle East, bordering the Mediterranean Sea, Lebanon, Syria, Egypt, Jordan, and the West Bank

Area (excludes occupied areas of Golan Heights, Gaza, and West Bank): about the size of New Jersey

total: 8,017 square miles (20,770 sq km)

land: 7,847 square miles (20,330 sq km)

water: 170 square miles (440 sq km)

Borders: Egypt, 165 miles (266 km); Gaza Strip, 32 miles (51 km); Jordan, 148 miles (238 km); Lebanon, 49 miles (79 km); Syria, 47 miles (76 km); West Bank, 191 miles (307 km)

Climate: hot and dry in south and east; more temperate along coast and in north

Terrain: Negev Desert in the south; low coastal plain; central mountains; Jordan Rift Valley

Elevation extremes:

highest point: Mount Meron—3,693 feet (1,208 meters)

lowest point: Dead Sea—1,349 feet (411 meters) below sea level

Natural hazards: drought, floods, earthquakes

Source: Adapted from CIA World Factbook, 2002.

town of Safad, there are thick forests. To the south and east, where the town of Nazareth lies, the vegetation is less dense.

THE JORDAN RIVER AND ITS VALLEY

Israel's only significant river is the Jordan, which flows south for about 200 miles (320 km). Its waters originate on the slopes of snow-capped Hermon, a mountain in the Golan Heights that rises to 9,232 feet (2,814 meters) above sea level at its highest point. The waters sink underground and emerge in springs that help form the Jordan's three major headwaters: the Dan, Banias, and Hasbani Rivers. Once these three sources combine, the Jordan River flows

Although the Jordan River has been celebrated in Bible stories and songs, the river is actually neither deep nor wide; in fact, in many places it is shallow enough to wade across. The Jordan River provides freshwater to the people of both Israel and Jordan.

into Lake Tiberias, Israel's largest freshwater reservoir. The river then emerges from the south of the lake to be joined from the east by a smaller river, the Yarmuk, which forms the border between Syria and Jordan. The river then falls sharply down into a part of the Great Rift Valley—a series of geological faults that extends from here all the way to Mozambique in southeastern Africa—and before long it is well below sea level. Eventually, what is left of the river, which is supplemented by mostly saline springs along its banks, flows into the landlocked Dead Sea.

The Dead Sea, so called because almost nothing can live in its extremely salty water, is the lowest point on earth, some 1,349 feet (411 meters) below sea level. Interestingly, the high salt content of the Dead Sea (which despite its name is actually a lake) makes it impossible for swimmers to sink!

Aside from the Jordan River—which itself is not at all "deep and wide," as the gospel songs say—there are no major rivers in Israel. Most Americans would call the Alexandroni, which flows to the

Mediterranean from the Carmel Heights, and the Yarkon, which flows east to west near Tel Aviv, mere streams or creeks.

Because of rainfall patterns, in some places Israel has riverbeds that are wet for only part of the year (almost always during the winter). These beds are known as wadis, and one of the most beautiful is near Lake Tiberias. Called Nahal Amud, it features pillars and caves carved by millennia of wind and rain. Rushing with water during the winter rains, the wadi, which slopes downward toward Lake Tiberias, is virtually dry in August.

The Great Rift Valley—which follows the Jordan River valley and then runs south across the Dead Sea and the Gulf of Aqaba—is a geologically active area, not just in Israel but also in East Africa. That is why there are warm and even hot springs in Israel (and

Mud-covered people on a beach in Israel. Spas like Hamat Gader and Ein Gedi, a fresh-water spring near the Dead Sea, attract health-conscious visitors who wish to bathe in waters said to have healing properties.

across the river in Jordan). One such place, today called Hamat Gader, was a spa for nobility during the ages when the land was part of the Roman and Byzantine empires. People still go there to bathe in its warm, mineral-rich waters, thought to have healing qualities. On the other hand, the entire area has historically been prone to earthquakes, some of them so major as to have virtually expunged civilizations. In ancient days, the Jewish high priest on the holiest day of the year, Yom Kippur, used to specifically pray that the residents of the Sharon Valley would not suffer their homes to turn into their tombs because of earthquakes.

HILLS, MOUNTAINS, AND OTHER FEATURES

To the west of the Jordan Valley (and also to the east, in Jordan) is a ridge of hills and old, eroded mountains that run north to south. On the east side of the hills, the Jordan Valley has two main subdivisions. One is the Beit Sha'an Valley, and the other, a very lush one, is called the Jezreel Valley. The Jezreel Valley, which lies at the foot of Mount Gilboa, is just east of a pass in the mountains where an ancient road runs from the valley toward the Mediterranean. At the entrance to that pass westward is Megiddo, an ancient fortress town where many battles were fought. (It is the root of the biblical word *Armageddon*.)

The Jordan Valley is quite hot in the summer, and it does not get as much rain as the areas farther to the west, especially between the western ridge of the hill country and the Mediterranean. The winds with the rain blow from west to east, and when they hit the hills, they drop moisture mainly on the western side (just as in the United States it rains more immediately west of the Rocky Mountains and the Appalachians than it does on the eastern sides of these ranges). In Israel, that means the coastal plain—called the Sharon Plain. That is where Israel's largest city, Tel Aviv, is located, and where the population is largely concentrated. It is also where the largest **aquifer** in the area, the Yarkon-Taninim aquifer, emerges from the hills at a place called Rosh Ha'ayin. Aquifers are very important sources of water for so dry a land.

Because the moist winds from the sea are so close to the hot desert on the east, and because of the elevation of the hills and mountains, at many times of the year parts of Israel are covered in dew in the evening and early morning. The dew (called *tal* in Hebrew) can be very heavy at times, and in certain places it even forms puddles. Dew is also very important to the environmental balance in a country as dry as Israel.

Atop the hill country near Israel's geographic north-south center lies the nation's capital and one of the oldest and most venerated cities in the world: Jerusalem. To the west of the city, and visible to the naked eye, are the coastal plain and the Mediterranean Sea. To the east can be seen the ancient town of Jericho, the Jordan Valley, and the Dead Sea. (Israel is so small that the human eye can see, from various spots in Jerusalem, all the way to the country's eastern and western limits.) South of Jerusalem, in the direction of the Negev, is the Judean Desert. Occasional freshwater springs erupt from the hills here and nourish life in the otherwise barren landscape. The most famous and beautiful of these is called Ein Gedi, which is near the Dead Sea. It is full of lush vegetation and many different kinds of animals, including ibex and leopards.

Most of the mountainous areas in Israel are formed of limestone, and over the years the rushing of underground water and erosion from rainwater have formed many caves in the mountains. Such caves are where the Essene sect hid what became known as the Dead Sea Scrolls, found accidentally by a shepherd boy in 1947.

Israel also has other fascinating geological features. One of them—called the *makhtesh*—is a crater-like formation found only in Israel and the Sinai Desert. The largest of these formations, Makhtesh Ramon, is located in the northern Negev south of

Jerusalem at night. Israel has controlled the entire city since 1967.

Beersheba. It is the remains of a large mountain that was hollowed out from within by volcanic activity and then collapsed on top of itself, leaving a kind of cluttered crater, full of symmetrically shaped basalt rocks and a variety of other rocky materials. Israel also contains sites that display an unusual wealth of ancient fossil life. One such site, Timneh, is located in the south near King Solomon's copper mines.

MICROCLIMATES

Because of the topography of the country, Israel has what climatologists call microclimates: virtually self-contained climate systems that cover only a small area. For example, from the highest point in the mountains of the Galilee, Mount Eval, eastward to the Jordan River, the land drops 5,000 feet (1,280 meters) in just 17 miles (28 km). Israel's microclimates are such that in January, it can be snowing in Jerusalem but dry and 75 degrees Fahrenheit (24 degrees Celsius) at the Dead Sea, just a few miles away.

Israel's microclimates give it a dizzying array of flora and fauna. Because the country is on the migration path of many birds, it is a bird-watcher's paradise. Over the course of a year, more than 500 bird species can be seen in Israel—more than any other country of comparable size in the world. Israel also has an extraordinary diversity of plant life, notably wildflowers. Many rare flowers exist in the northern Negev, and after the first autumn or winter rain, what seems an entirely barren landscape explodes with color.

A DEARTH OF NATURAL RESOURCES

On the other hand, Israel does not have many economically valuable natural resources. It has virtually no deposits of oil or natural gas, but some copper. Potash, bromine, manganese, and sulfur are mined along the shores of the Dead Sea, which Israel shares with Jordan. But Israel's economy depends not so much on its natural resources as on its human capital, its trade in high-tech goods, its tourist industry, and the support of Jewish and other well-wishers around the world.

Only about 17 percent of Israel's land is arable, or suitable for agriculture, and some of that just barely so because of the lack of water and erratic rainfall patterns. Israel has gone to great effort and expense to use what water is does have to maximum efficiency; it boasts perhaps the most sophisticated hydrological infrastructure in the world. (Israel has also traditionally had disputes with its neighbors over water ownership and usage, but for many years it cooperated with Jordan on water and other environmental issues, even before the two nations signed a peace treaty in 1994.) Despite limited arable land, Israel grows most of its own food, and its fruit and vegetables are of very high quality. In the early years of the state, Israel was a major exporter of citrus fruits and flowers to European and other countries. Israelis also raise animals—chickens and sheep more than cows—but the country imports

An Arab boy riding a donkey leads a herd of sheep through the rural Jordan Valley.

some of its meats and grains.

Israel's climate and water situation have made it for thousands of years a land where sedentary agriculture was possible only in some places, and at some risk of failure, and animal husbandry made sense in other places. In Israel one can see terraces on the sides of many hills that look almost natural, but have in fact been made by thousands of years of use by shepherds driving their sheep and goats to and from pasture. One can also see tree crops that do not require a lot of water to thrive: olives, pistachios, and almonds, for example.

Israel today also has sophisticated hothouse fruit industries, some on collective farms called kibbutzim and moshavim, where mangoes, guava, papayas, bananas, and other tropical fruits are grown. Israel also has many artificial ponds where fish are raised and harvested commercially.

A CROSSROADS

Israel is located at a geographic crossroads—at the western limits of the Asian continent, very close to northeast Africa—yet at the same time it is part of the Mediterranean world with its European influences. Throughout history, the region has been coveted by a succession of civilizations from Asia and Europe.

Given its location, one would expect to see brisk movement of people, goods, and services through modern Israel. Yet that is not exactly the case, and the primary reason is the strained if not hostile relations between Israel and the Arab countries of the region. Israel has peace treaties with two of its neighbors, Egypt and Jordan. It lacks such treaties with the other two countries with which it shares borders, Syria and Lebanon, and with the remaining 17 Arab countries. None of these 19 Arab countries recognizes Israel or has diplomatic relations with it, and some, such as Iraq and Libya, consider themselves at war with Israel. Furthermore, Israel has extremely difficult relations with Palestinian Arabs in the West Bank and Gaza.

Israelis therefore trade with and travel to Europe and other places in Asia and North America more than they do the countries nearest to them. Many Israelis study and some even live in the United States. Turkey is a favorite tourist and vacation spot for Israelis because it is beautiful, close, relatively inexpensive, and full of friendly people.

Because of its culture and location, Israel remains a link between the West and the East—yet it is not entirely one or the other. Perhaps in future years Israel will be more fully integrated, economically and otherwise, in its own region.

Israeli Jews face the western wall (sometimes called the Wailing Wall) of what was once the Jewish Temple in Jerusalem. The western wall has traditionally been a sacred symbol of mourning over the destruction of the Temple in A.D. 70 and the Jewish Diaspora.

History

There are two ways to think about the history of Israel. If one focuses on the majority of the people who live in Israel today—on the nation, properly speaking—then one needs to understand something about Jewish history. If one focuses not on the people but on the physical place itself—on the country as opposed to the nation—then one needs to understand something about the broader imperial history of the Middle East. Of course, it is the intersection of these two ways of thinking about Israel's history that offers the best, most complete view.

As a center and crossroads of ancient civilizations in the Near East, the land of Israel has been inhabited by humans since before recorded history. There are many archaeological sites in Israel that record human communal life more than 12,000 years ago. The oldest name for the land was Canaan, which is mentioned in the Bible and other ancient sources.

The basic Bible story is, of course, very well known in Christian cultures like America, but it is worth taking a moment to sketch it here.

JEWISH HISTORY TO THE ROMAN ERA

According to the Bible story, the beginning of the Jewish people starts with Abraham, who was the first person to recognize and proclaim the oneness of God. About 6,000 years ago, God called on Abraham to leave his home in Mesopotamia (a place called Ur in Chaldea) and go to Canaan. When he got there, the land was inhabited by a number of tribes and people, including the Hittites, who had come from the north. Abraham's grandson, Jacob, had 12 sons, whose descendants became the 12 tribes of Israel. One of those sons, Joseph, ended up in Egypt, where he helped the Egyptian pharaoh avert the disaster of a major famine. During that famine, the rest of Joseph's brothers and their families left Canaan to live in Goshen, a part of Egypt. Then, as the story goes, the Israelites—so called after Jacob's second name, Israel (which means "he who struggles with God"), given to him by an

This 18th-century painting by Austrian artist Giovan Battista Lama depicts Abraham preparing to sacrifice his son Isaac as ordered by God. Jews consider Abraham to be a patriarch, or father of the Hebrew people; he is also revered by Muslims and Christians.

angel—were enslaved in Egypt by a new pharaoh who had forgotten Joseph's service. Several hundred years later, Moses arose and led the Israelites out of bondage in Egypt, in 1220 B.C. Eventually, the Israelites made their way back to Canaan, the Promised Land, which came to be known as Israel.

There is little, if any, independent historical corroboration for the Bible story or the origins of the Jews and early Jewish history to this point. What happened next does have grounding in archaeology, however. Forty years after the exodus from Egypt, the Israelites entered Canaan under Moses' successor, Joshua, and slowly began to conquer the entire country. This took a long time, during which the people were ruled by a succession of prophets. By the time of Israel's first king, Saul, in about 1080 B.C., the Israelites controlled most of what is today Israel. Later, under Israel's most famous kings, David and his son Solomon, the Israelites controlled a larger area, including parts of what is today Lebanon, Syria, Jordan, and even Iraq.

After Solomon's death in 933 B.C., the country was divided into two kingdoms, the northern part called Israel and the southern part Judah (after its largest tribe). The northern part of the country fell away from the law that the Bible says God gave to the people of Israel. Eventually, in 722 B.C, the Northern Kingdom was conquered and destroyed by the Assyrians, who carried the people away in captivity. The fate of the 10 so-called lost tribes of Israel is still a staple of speculation and anthropological investigation.

In 586 B.C., the Babylonian Empire conquered the Kingdom of Judah (from whence comes the word *Jew*). The Holy Temple in Jerusalem, constructed under the reign of King Solomon, was destroyed, and the exile of the Jews of Judea (as the land was now called) began. This marked the end of the first major period of Jewish independence in what is today Israel—a period known as the First Commonwealth.

Within just 60 years, however, Persia conquered Babylonia. Under the Persian king, Cyrus, the Jews were restored to their land and began building a second Holy Temple. But not all the Jews returned, and important academies for Jewish learning grew up in Babylonia. During this time, the main commentary to the Torah (the first five books of the Hebrew Bible)—called the Talmud—was written. It was also in Babylonia that the Jews picked up the writing script that is now used for Hebrew.

Before long, the Second Commonwealth was established, and again Jews ruled most of what is today the land of Israel. The Second Commonwealth lasted for many centuries, until the Macedonians under Alexander the Great conquered the whole region in 331 B.C. Alexander, who was much influenced by classical Greek civilization, spread the ideals of Greek culture to the lands he conquered. During the post-Alexander period of Greek-inspired rule, called the Hellenistic era, the Jews enjoyed much autonomy and the Temple continued to function, along with the religious life of the people. But within three centuries Hellenistic culture gave way to the rising Roman Empire.

ROMAN CONQUEST

By 63 B.C., the land of Israel was controlled by Rome, although the Jewish people still had much independence, most famously under King Herod. But the Jews rebelled against Rome in A.D. 66, as Rome gained new leaders who wished to consolidate and tighten Roman rule. The second Temple was destroyed in the year 70, and after they crushed a further revolt, the Bar Kokhba Rebellion, in 135, the Romans exiled the bulk of the Jewish population. The Roman general Titus plundered Jerusalem and brought to Rome many of its treasures. An arch—called Titus' arch—was built, with carvings of the victory procession and the inscription, "Judea capta" (Judea is captured).

Out of pique at the Jews' rebellion, which proved much harder to put down than they had anticipated, the Romans called the country after the Jews' traditional enemies, the Philistines, who lived along the Mediterranean coast to the south of the ancient port city of Jaffa (which today adjoins Tel Aviv). That is how, and when, the land first came to be called Palestine.

It is at this point, in the year 135, that the history of the Jews separates from the history of the country. For the roughly 1,600 years before that, the histories were parallel.

PALESTINE UNDER VARIOUS EMPIRES

Palestine eventually became part of the Eastern Roman Empire (later called the Byzantine Empire) after the Roman Empire split into eastern and western halves in the late fourth century. It remained part of the Byzantine Empire for hundreds of years, during which many of the people living there became Christians.

The country was then conquered by tribes from the Arabian Peninsula professing a new religion, Islam, in the year 638. With the exception of the short interlude of the Crusades, when European invaders held parts of Palestine (including Jerusalem) in the 12th century, the land remained under a succession of Islamic empires, first mainly Arab (Umayyad), then partly Persian (Abassid), and still later others (Fatimid, Mameluke) that were

This stone carving—a detail from a church in Jerusalem—shows Jesus carrying his cross. Jesus was a Jew who lived and died in Israel some 2,000 years ago; his followers, believing he was the long-awaited Messiah, established a religion based on his teachings that quickly spread throughout the world—Christianity.

Egyptian or Turkic. In the early part of the 16th century, the Ottoman Turks conquered the entire Middle East. From 1517 to 1917, the Ottoman Turks ruled Palestine. At the end of World War I, when the Ottoman Empire collapsed, Palestine became a British **Mandate** under the new League of Nations.

During all this time, some Jews lived in the land, mainly in Jerusalem and three other cities of particular historical and religious significance to Jews: Safad, Hebron, and Tiberias. But by the 12th century, most people in the country were Muslims, although many Orthodox Christians also remained. Eventually, Arabic became the dominant language of the country.

Before the 20th century, people tended to identify themselves by religion, by the locality in which they lived, and by their extended family (clan, or tribe). Under the Ottoman Empire, the *millet* (national) system allowed religious leaders legal autonomy over their peoples for many purposes. Western ideas of nationalism, the nation-state, and abstract concepts of citizenship did not exist.

The Ottoman Turks did not administer Palestine as a single province, and they did not call it Palestine. The term *Palestine* became a geographical rather than a political concept, like the term *Scandinavia*. The northern part of the country was ruled most of the time as part of the *vilayet* (province) of Damascus (in Syria). Jerusalem was a separate administrative entity. The southern parts of the country, in the desert, were not really administered at all, but rather were left to the nomadic Bedouin tribes. The far south of the country, near Gaza and the Red Sea, was effectively part of Egypt, which nominally fell under Ottoman rule.

JEWS IN EUROPE AND THE RISE OF ANTI-SEMITISM

Meanwhile, throughout the centuries after A.D. 135, the exiled Jews became one of the most unusual phenomena in all history. Dispersed in many lands—including Italy, Spain, Portugal, France,

Germany, Poland, Russia, and the Ottoman Empire—the Jews nevertheless managed to remain psychologically one people because of the portable nature of their religious culture. Hebrew and Aramaic (a tongue adopted by ancient Jews after the Babylonian exile) became languages of prayer and study only; Jews came to speak the languages of the countries in which they lived.

It is very difficult to generalize about the experience of the Jews over so many centuries in so many countries. But basically, although a certain number of Jews intermarried with other peoples in the many lands in which they settled—and, in the process, some Jews assimilated into the larg-er society and ceased being Jews, while some members of the larger society converted to Judaism—Jews usually stayed apart from the general popula-tion. This was in part because the Jews wished to maintain their unique religious beliefs and traditions, and in part because the general popula-tion within which the Jews lived usually also wished to keep separate from them. Jews

An Ottoman tower, Khan al-Umdan, located in Akko (Acre). The Ottoman Empire ruled the area called Palestine from 1517 until 1917, when a British army forced the Turks to withdraw from Jerusalem.

therefore formed a community within a community almost every-where they lived.

Jews were usually, but not always, urban dwellers engaged in crafts and commerce, for they were often not allowed to own land, and thus could not become farmers. Because of this, and because of the nature of Jewish religious culture, Jews stressed education generation after generation—which helps to account for how well Jews have done at intellectual and professional pursuits.

In some places and at some times—for example, Muslim Spain between the 8th and the 15th centuries—Jewish communities thrived. Particularly in Islamic lands, Jews lived side by side with their neighbors, and while they were second-class citizens formal-ly, they rarely suffered violent persecution. Toleration also existed at various times in many European Christian lands, but overall

During the years of the Diaspora, persecution of Jews was common, particularly in Europe. This Italian painting from the 15th century shows a Jewish family being burned at the stake.

Jews faced more persecution in Europe than under Muslim rule.

As European lands evolved from agriculture-based feudal societies toward the more commercial and urban civilizations of the early modern period, non-Jews came increasingly to resent the economic niches Jews had filled. Combined with religious prejudices, this economic resentment gave rise to modern anti-Semitism. In many European countries, Jews formed the most prominent non-native, or non-national, non-Christian group, and so politics sometimes came to be organized around opposition to the Jews. Whole Jewish communities were attacked and expelled from many European countries, including England, France, and, after they became Christian countries, Spain and Portugal in 1492—the same year Christopher Columbus sailed to America (with a Jewish mapmaker named Abraham Zaputo).

Anti-Semitism in Europe got worse after the 16th century. By then, many Jews had moved farther east, into the Russian Empire. Some had fled persecution. Some were invited—for example, by Polish nobles in the 16th century—to help build up the culture and economy of the country. Some migrated for economic opportunity.

As the idea of nationalism arose in the 18th century and spread in the 19th, Jews came increasingly to be seen as foreign elements in new national states. This was magnified in some cases by religious prejudice against the Jews as "Christ killers." Although terrible violence against Jewish communities had periodically erupted in pre-modern times—for example, in Germany during the period of the Crusades, and in England in places like York—in modern times, violent persecution became more widespread, more organized, and more frequent. In Poland, for example, the Chmelnitsky massacres of 1648–1655 killed nearly one-third of the entire Jewish population of that country.

Naturally, given their outsider status, higher levels of education, and vulnerability, Jews gravitated to places and toward political philosophies where ethnic-based nationalism was weak. As time passed, Jews tended to embrace progressive, Enlightenment ideas that stressed equality and freedom for all, rather than the group-centered ideas of nationalism. Jews came to be seen in many countries as vanguards of modern political movements, and they thus became the enemy of all conservative, reactionary, and anti-modern political currents in Europe. Almost every right-wing nationalist party and political movement in Europe throughout the 19th and 20th centuries was to some extent, tacitly or explicitly, anti-Semitic.

Jews watched this development with great fear. They had basically four reactions to it. Where it was possible for them to become first-class citizens in liberal states, such as Britain and France, many Jews tried to assimilate into the general culture. Some converted to Christianity, but others tried to reform their Jewish heritage to make it conform to the new national ethos.

In very conservative places like the Russian Empire, however, it was not possible for Jews to fit into the larger society, so many chose a second reaction to anti-Semitism: emigration. Large numbers of Jews from the Russian Empire went to America in the 19th and early 20th centuries. (Most American Jews today descend from that wave of immigrants.) Some Jews also went to Palestine, in what was called the First Aliyah ("going up").

A third reaction to anti-Semitism in Europe was for Jews to become socialist revolutionaries and try to overthrow the existing forms of government. Some Jews, and others, believed that entirely new kinds of governments ruling over new social and economic systems would eliminate anti-Semitism. In significant numbers Jews joined socialist and communist parties.

A fourth reaction—at first by only a handful of Jews—rejected assimilation, immigration to other non-Jewish countries such as the United States, and revolution. This group was influenced by the idea of nationalism. They witnessed the unification of Italy and Germany into new national states in or around 1870. They saw the stirrings of ethnic nationalism in the culturally and linguistically diverse Habsburg Empire (also called the Austro-Hungarian Empire). In the face of these developments, a few Jews asked themselves why the Jewish people couldn't reunite, thereby symbolically rejoining their ancient history—as the recently reunified Italy had harked back to its ancient Roman roots.

EARLY YEARS OF THE ZIONIST MOVEMENT

From such thoughts arose the idea of modern Jewish nationalism, called ***Zionism***. The first Zionists were men like Moses Hess, Judah Alkalai, Asher Ginzberg (Ehad Ha'am), and Leo Pinsker. But the man who put the idea of Zionism on the mental map of the Jewish people, and who had the energy and organizational skills to establish it as a movement, was Theodor Herzl. In 1897 Herzl organized the first Zionist Congress, which met in Basel, Switzerland. Its aim was to re-create a Jewish national homeland, and before long it became clear that the only logical and practical place this could happen was the ancient land of Israel, which was then still called Palestine.

Herzl tried to interest the great powers in Zionism as a solution to their own "Jewish problem," as it was called. At that time, because Palestine was ruled by the Ottoman Empire, Herzl tried to enlist the help of European leaders in persuading the Turks to let Jews settle in Palestine. He also attempted directly to persuade the Turks, who were trying to reform and modernize their country, that the Jews would help them do so.

Herzl did not have much success. Not only did the great powers and the Turks not respond positively to his pleas, but most Jews in western Europe thought Herzl was dangerous and crazy. They regarded his plan as a fantasy, and they worried that the idea of

אִם תִּרְצוּ אֵין זוֹ אַגָּדָה

Theodor Herzl (1860–1904) was one of the most influential leaders of the Zionist movement. His 1896 book *Der Judenstaat* (The Jewish State) argued that anti-Semitism was a problem that could be solved only if Jews had their own state. Another of his books, *Altneuland* (Old New Land), was a utopian novel that described what life might be like in a Jewish state. Herzl died young, but remained an inspiration to other Zionists; in 1949, after the State of Israel was created, his remains were exhumed, brought to Jerusalem, and reinterred there.

modern Jewish nationalism would cast doubt on their loyalty to the individual European countries in which they lived.

Most Orthodox Jews also opposed Zionism because it was a mainly secular movement and they believed that religious Jews should be waiting for God to redeem them. That, they believed, would happen with the coming of the Messiah. A few wealthy west European Jews gave money to the Zionist movement to aid impoverished and persecuted Jews of eastern Europe who wanted to settle in Palestine, but when Herzl died in 1904 at the age of only 44, his movement was divided, small, weak, and bereft of any significant success.

Among the Zionist movement's other problems was the fact that Arab nationalism had begun to infiltrate into the Ottoman Empire as well. In 1905 a group called the Young Turks tried to seize control of the Ottoman government to more quickly and radically modernize it. Instead of thinking of themselves only or mainly as Muslims, they began to think of themselves in national terms, as Turks. By extension, the Arabs of the Ottoman Empire soon began to wonder: If the rulers who speak Turkish are now thinking of themselves as members of a Turkish nation, then what are we who speak Arabic? Their answer was that they would become second-class citizens inside a Turkish empire, and a few Arabs—mostly educated urban-dwellers, and many Christian Arabs—began to think of Arab nationalism. This Arab nationalism took two forms: nationalism involving specific areas, such as Egypt, Syria, or Iraq; and nationalism that included all Arabs, called Pan-Arabism.

In Palestine, where there were about 600,000 Arabs at the turn of the 20th century, the idea of Palestine as a political entity, or a specifically Palestinian nationalism, did not exist. That is why some Christian Zionists (Christians who for theological reasons favored the ingathering of Jews in Palestine) and early Jewish Zionists used to say of Palestine, "For a people without a land, a land without a people." (They meant "people" in terms of a self-conscious national group—which at that point described Jews but not Palestinian Arabs.)

THE WORLD WARS AND ZIONISM

This, then, is the historical background for the revolutionary changes that occurred between the beginning of World War I and the years just after the end of World War II. The story is complicated, and what follows is a somewhat simplified version of events.

The First World War, which broke out in 1914, pitted Britain, France, Russia, and eventually the United States against Germany, Austria-Hungary, and the Ottoman Empire. To undermine the Ottoman Turks, the British fomented an Arab uprising in Ottoman territories. In return for Arab help, the British promised that, after the war, they would take the Arab lands away from the Turks and allow an independent Arab state to arise.

At the same time, the British also tried to enlist the support of Jews living within Germany and the Ottoman Empire, hoping to inspire uprisings or acts of sabotage. In addition, there were many Christian Zionists in elite British circles, and the head of the Zionist movement, Chaim Weizmann, was a brilliant chemist who helped the British create explosives crucial to their war effort. In return, the British government in November 1917 issued the Balfour Declaration, a promise to facilitate "a national home for the Jewish people" in Palestine after the war. Nothing was said explicitly about a sovereign independent state, but that is what was understood to be the eventual plan.

Britain's promise to the Arabs, specifically to the Hashemite family that ruled in Mecca in what is today Saudi Arabia, was territorially vague. It did not include Palestine, but the borders of Palestine had not even been defined. The promise to the Zionists was more specific—it mentioned Palestine—but, again, no borders were specified. However, the biblical phrase "from Dan to Beersheba" was what the British imagined to be Palestine. And in Anglican churches and Bibles, maps of the Holy Land were plentiful, so the British elite thought they knew more or less what Palestine meant as a geographical concept.

At the same time, however, the British had made a secret deal with their other allies, mainly France, but also including Russia and later Italy, to divide up Ottoman lands after the war. This was called the Sykes-Picot accord, and it was negotiated, with a map, in 1916.

There are many myths about the Sykes-Picot accord. One is that it excluded the idea of an independent Arab state after World War I, making the British promise to the Arabs seem like an outright deception. In fact, the original map of the secret agreement shows zones for France and Britain clearly marked out (France in Lebanon and coastal Syria, Britain in Palestine and Mesopotamia), but the majority of the inland territory, called zone A and zone B, is set aside for an "independent Arab state." Those three words are actually written on the map. These areas are noted to be under French and British influence, respectively, but how much influence London or Paris really expected or wanted to exert is still a matter of study and debate.

In any event, during the war, the British actually conquered Palestine and Mesopotamia, and France did not. The French suspected the British of using the Arabs and the Zionists to take advantage of them. After the war, conflict and competition between the French and the British made obsolete the Sykes-Picot map,

The Balfour Declaration

The following is the text of the famous letter sent by Arthur James Balfour, the British foreign secretary, to Lionel Walter Rothschild, head of the British Zionist Federation, on November 2, 1917.

Dear Lord Rothschild,

I have much pleasure in conveying to you, on behalf of His Majesty's Government, the following declaration of sympathy with Jewish Zionist aspirations which has been submitted to, and approved by, the Cabinet.

"His Majesty's Government view with favour the establishment in Palestine of a national home for the Jewish people, and will use their best endeavours to facilitate the achievement of this object, it being clearly understood that nothing shall be done which may prejudice the civil and religious rights of existing non-Jewish communities in Palestine, or the rights and political status enjoyed by Jews in any other country."

I should be grateful if you would bring this declaration to the knowledge of the Zionist Federation.

Yours sincerely,
Arthur James Balfour

World leaders sign the Treaty of Versailles in 1919, officially ending the First World War. After the war the League of Nations, an international organization similar to the modern United Nations, divided the former Ottoman territories into mandates ruled by Great Britain and France. The British received the mandate for Palestine.

except in very general terms.

The Versailles Treaty of 1919, which officially ended World War I, established the League of Nations and divided the former Arab domains of the Ottoman Empire into international protectorates, called mandates, that were assigned to the British and the French. France received the mandate for Syria (and Lebanon), Britain the mandate for Mesopotamia (Iraq) and Palestine. After three years of negotiation and argument among the British, the French, and the Zionists, the borders of Palestine were decided, and the provisions of the Balfour Declaration were written into the Mandate provisions.

Because of the war, the British and French occupations, and the higher profile and political successes of the Zionist movement, the

Arabs of Palestine began to hone their concept of their own national identity. In the early 1920s, they began to organize themselves in opposition to both the British Mandate and the Zionists. The Arabs fomented violence against the growing Jewish population, and British Mandate authorities were caught in the middle. Arabs outside of Palestine tended to sympathize with their fellow Arabs, and a few tried to help them.

As time passed, relations between the Jewish and Arab communities in Palestine worsened. The Arabs thought the Jews had no right to come to Palestine, at least not as equals to Muslims. They worried that the Jews, because they were from Europe, were better educated, and had more capital at hand, would become more powerful than the Arabs. They wanted the British to restrict Jewish immigration to Palestine. The Jews did not want trouble with the Arabs, and most Zionists believed that their building up and investing in the land would be good for the Arabs, too. Indeed, during the 1930s there was considerable in-migration of Arabs to Palestine because of the relatively good economy there. But the Zionists, helped by contributions mainly from Jews in America, were buying land from mostly absentee Arab landlords, and that was forcing Arab peasants off the land.

The Zionist movement at the time was heavily influenced by socialist ideology, and its aim was to re-create a normal, as opposed to exilic, Jewish society in Palestine, with laborers and agriculturalists as well as professionals and merchants—something that was not possible in exile. So the Zionists tried not to hire Arab laborers because they did not want to "exploit" them; they wanted Jews to do the hard labor, natural for an ideology that saw itself as part of an international labor socialist movement. The local Arabs knew nothing of socialist ideology. Nor could they have been expected to understand the long and unusual history that had led to the rise of Zionism. So they saw the unwillingness of the **Yishuv**—the name for the reestablished Jewish community in Palestine—to hire them as unjustified exclusion.

In 1933 Adolf Hitler came to power in Germany. Soon afterward, his Nazi regime began restricting the rights of German Jews. In November 1938 the first major manifestation of anti-Jewish violence in Nazi Germany—called *Kristallnacht* ("the Night of Broken Glass")—occurred.

At the same time that the rise of Nazism threatened Jews in Europe, Arab anti-Jewish violence in Palestine intensified. In 1936 the Arab Revolt—a violent uprising that included attacks on Jews as well as British Mandate authorities—broke out. The Palestinian

The dictator Adolf Hitler (1889–1945) came to power in Germany in 1933. That same year, Germany began to pass laws that discriminated against German Jews, such as a one-day boycott of Jewish-owned shops. By 1936 Jews had been deprived of German citizenship by the Nuremberg Laws and were not permitted to participate in elections. After government-promoted violence against German Jews in November 1938 (Kristallnacht, or "the Night of Broken Glass"), Jews were no longer allowed to own businesses or property, and were segregated from the rest of German society.

Arabs, whose uprising would last until 1939, sought an end to Jewish immigration, the banning of all future land sales to Jews, and the establishment of an Arab government in Palestine.

Because of their own strategic concerns, the British were inclined to appease the Palestinian Arabs. A war with Germany loomed, and to the extent possible, the British wanted to keep the Arabs (who were far more numerous than the Jews) on their side. In 1933 and again in 1936, the British sharply restricted Jewish immigration to Palestine.

The Zionists complained that such restrictions violated the Balfour Declaration, which had been written into Britain's Palestine Mandate obligations. They saw that just when the dangers to Jews were rising in Europe, Palestine's role as a sanctuary was being shut off. Fearing the worst, David Ben-Gurion, who had succeeded Chaim Weizmann as leader of the Zionist movement, authorized secret deals with the Nazis to ransom Jews out of Europe. He also authorized violations of the British immigration restrictions. Meanwhile, smaller, splinter groups within the Zionist movement began attacking British soldiers in Palestine.

When World War II broke out on September 1, 1939, with Germany's invasion of Poland, Ben-Gurion proclaimed that the Jews of Palestine would fight British restrictions on immigration as if there were no war, and would fight the war on Britain's side against the Nazis as if there were no immigration restrictions. The Palestinian Arabs, meanwhile, took Germany's side; their leader, Haj Amin al-Husseini, spent much of the war in Berlin, broadcasting pro-Nazi propaganda in Arabic to the Arab world.

Zionist efforts to save the Jews of Europe—whom the Nazis systematically murdered—fell very far short. While some Jews did escape to Palestine and elsewhere, the majority perished at the hands of the Nazis and their allies. After the war ended in 1945, the extent of the horror became clear: under the Nazis' program to wipe

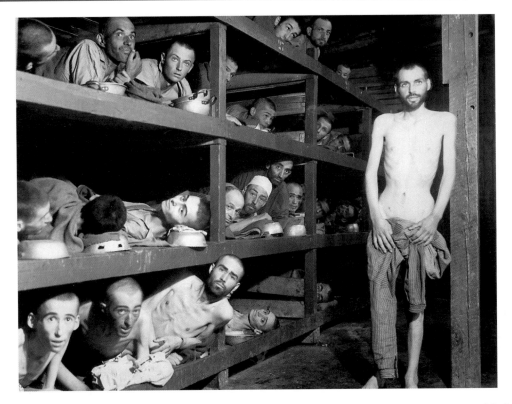

From 1940 to 1945, as Nazi Germany spread its power across Europe, Hitler and his minions ordered the imprisonment and enslavement of millions of Jews in concentration camps. Those who were old or infirm were usually killed outright, while healthy men and women were forced to work in the camps, often contributing to the Nazi war machine. By the end of the war the Holocaust had claimed the lives of approximately 6 million Jews. Pictured here are malnourished slave laborers in the Buchenwald concentration camp, liberated by U.S. troops on April 16, 1945.

out the entire Jewish population of Europe—an act that inspired a new term, *genocide*—about 6 million Jews, of whom almost 1.5 million were children younger than age 13, had been killed.

As the world learned of this catastrophe, which soon became known as the Holocaust, its sympathies turned strongly toward the Jews and the Zionists. Assimilated Jews in Western countries (especially Reform Jews) who had previously been opponents of Zionism now saw what their opposition had allowed to happen.

Across war-ravaged Europe, meanwhile, tens of thousands of Jewish survivors languished in displaced-person camps. The vast majority wanted to go to Palestine, but the British government refused to allow them to enter, despite pleas from U.S. president Harry Truman.

ESTABLISHMENT OF THE STATE OF ISRAEL

Meanwhile, the British were losing control of India, and their rule over Palestine had been intended mainly to protect their route to and from that important colony. So by 1947, Palestine had become less important strategically to Britain. In addition, Jewish and Arab violence against British rule in Palestine rose dramatically after 1945, further eroding Britain's desire to stay. Eventually, the British gave up and turned the problem over to the newly formed United Nations. A committee studied the matter and decided that two states, one Jewish and one Arab, should be established in Palestine. A map of a partitioned Palestine was drawn up.

In November 1947 the United Nations General Assembly voted on the partition plan, and with both the United States and the Soviet Union in favor, the plan passed. The Zionists did not like the map, but they accepted the idea of partition. The Arabs, however, both inside and outside Palestine, rejected the idea of any Jewish state in Palestine ever, in any borders whatsoever. Almost immediately after the UN vote on partition, a communal war in Palestine erupted. Palestinian Arabs (with support from Arab countries in the region) attacked Jews and Jewish settlements, and Jewish groups retaliated by attacking Arabs.

The Arab states publicly threatened war if a Jewish state in Palestine were proclaimed. But one Arab country, Transjordan (which later became Jordan), secretly made a deal with the Zionists to prevent a Palestinian Arab state from coming into being. In return for acquiescing in the creation of Israel, the Jordanians

The State of Israel's first leader, David Ben-Gurion, was born David Gruen in Poland in 1884. Like many Zionists, Ben-Gurion, whose first language was Yiddish, changed his name to give it Hebraic roots. This was intended to emphasize the new chapter in Jewish history that Zionism was writing: a reconnection of the Jewish people with their past in their own land.

would take the area set aside for the Palestinian Arabs west of the Jordan River. However, they could not agree about Jerusalem, which both Israel and Transjordan wanted but which the UN committee envisioned as an international zone.

When the British flag was lowered in Palestine for the last time and Ben-Gurion proclaimed the independence of the State of Israel on May 14, 1948, it was the signal for war. Armies from five Arab nations—Egypt, Syria, Transjordan, Lebanon, and Iraq—attacked the new Jewish state.

The military situation seemed to favor the Arabs greatly. Not only was Israel surrounded by hostile Arab nations, but also, with fewer than a million adult residents, it was at a huge numerical disadvantage. Yet despite some early gains by the Arabs, Israel managed not simply to survive, but actually to expand the territory under its control beyond the original partition boundaries, before the fighting had ended in January 1949.

Several factors help account for the seemingly miraculous defense of Israel at its birth. First, the Jews were fighting for their lives, so their motivation and morale were high. They were also well organized. The Arabs, on the other hand, did not coordinate their efforts—in large part because the various Arab leaders were jealous of one another and had different goals. Transjordan, for example, fought not to destroy Israel but to take the Arab part of Palestine for itself.

In addition to firmly establishing the State of Israel and changing the political map of the Middle East, the 1948–49 war produced a large number of Palestinian Arab refugees. Of a pre-partition population of about 1 million, some 750,000 Palestinian Arabs fled the territory that would become Israel. Arabs say this is because the

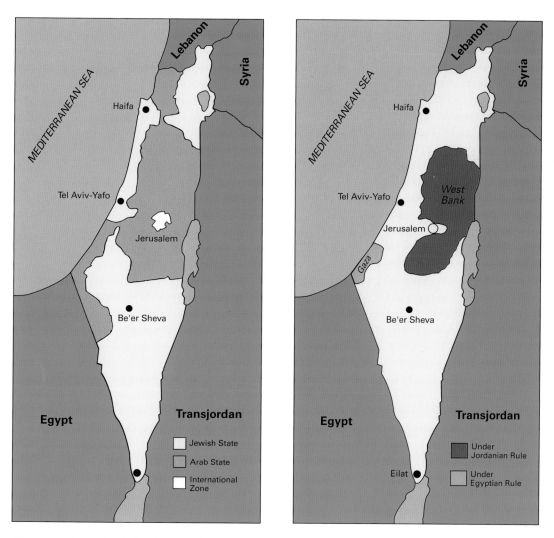

The map on the left shows the United Nations' 1947 plan to partition Palestine into Zionist and Arab states—a plan virulently opposed by the Arabs. When the British withdrew from Palestine in May 1948, the Arab forces attacked, determined to drive the Jews out of the country. The map on the right shows the boundaries of Israel at the end of the 1948–49 War of Independence.

Israeli immigrants settle at Tarshiha, in the Galilee, in houses abandoned by Palestinian Arabs who fled the country during the 1948–49 period.

Jews forced them out at gunpoint. Zionists claim that Arab leaders told the Palestinians to stand aside while their armies destroyed the Jews. In truth, neither of these explanations holds up very well.

Only in a few strategic places were Arabs forced from their homes by Israeli soldiers. And only in one or two isolated cases is there any evidence that Arab leaders told Arabs to temporarily vacate their homes. Rather, the flight of Palestinian Arabs is mainly attributable to their desire to escape the violence; wars almost always produce refugees. Many of the refugees were from the Palestinian Arab elite—some, fearing difficult times ahead, had begun exporting their money and their families before the outbreak of the war, which contributed to the collapse of the local economy. Also, a significant number of Arabs in Palestine were recent arrivals from other countries, and these people often had family outside of Palestine with whom they could live. These facts explain why the approximately 200,000 to 250,000 Arabs who did not leave Israel tended to be the most rural—those whose wealth was not liquid, who had nowhere else to go, and who lived on more marginal lands that were not central to the Zionist land purchase plan.

The refusal of all the Arabs to accept the UN partition had cost the Palestinian Arabs most dearly. No Palestinian Arab homeland existed. Israel now occupied some of the territory originally set aside for that purpose; Egypt had taken a strip of land known as Gaza along the Mediterranean coast; and Transjordan had seized territory to the west of the Jordan River, including East Jerusalem (Israel was in control of the newer, western part of the city). The Jordanian king, Abdullah, anxious to expunge the name Palestine from the map (and along with it, the nationalist aspirations of Palestinian Arabs), renamed the area the West Bank. In July 1951 the king was assassinated by a Palestinian nationalist.

As for Israel, as soon as it had established and defended itself in war, its main aims were threefold: security against further Arab aggression; immigration of as many Jews as possible to Israel; and the building of a new Jewish culture in line with the Zionist movement's democratic socialist ideology. The first two tasks put a high premium on the nature of Israel's foreign relations. The last put a premium on domestic energies. We take up both of these dimensions of Israeli politics and society in subsequent chapters.

Chaim Weizmann (1874–1952), a longtime leader of the Zionist movement and the first president of Israel, cuts a ribbon with golden scissors during a ceremony marking his first visit to Jerusalem as head of the Israeli government in February 1949.

Society, Politics, and Security

In most cases, it is appropriate to discuss the society, politics, and foreign policy aspects of a country separately from one another. While this approach can be taken with Israel, it is much easier to discuss these three aspects of national life together because in Israel they have been very tightly intertwined ever since the establishment and consolidation of the Yishuv in the period after World War I, and remain so to the present day. Since Israel has been technically, and often literally, at war since its founding in 1948, its domestic and foreign politics are almost impossible to separate. Bringing more Jews to the country—that is, the very formation of the society—was always seen in political and national security terms, as well. For these reasons, this book differs in its organization from the other volumes in the series.

In this chapter, we will sketch out briefly Israel's social and political development from Mandate times through the establishment of the basic institutions of the state after 1948. Chapter 5 will take the story until 1977. Chapter 6 will then discuss the period between 1978 through the January 2003 Israeli election.

DEVELOPMENT OF ZIONIST INSTITUTIONS

In November 1917, at the time of the Balfour Declaration, there were only about 90,000 Jews in Palestine, compared with about 500,000 Arabs. So the main priority for the Zionist movement was to encourage and support the migration of Jews to Palestine. To build the Jewish community in Palestine, the Yishuv, the movement needed to develop the country economically. To do that, it needed money—to buy land, build towns, and develop both the

The Histadrut pavilion at the fairground in Tel Aviv, 1934. The Histadrut was founded in December 1920 as a trade union for Jewish workers in Palestine; by 1927 it represented about three-fourths of the Jewish labor force in the region.

educational and the physical infrastructure of the country. To raise money, the Zionist Executive (the leadership, drawn from the various socialist factions or parties) established the Jewish National Fund (JNF). The connection between Zionists living in the Yishuv and their supporters around the world was institutionalized in the World Zionist Organization (WZO).

In the main, the early Zionist movement thought of itself as a coalition of socialist political parties that wished to form a state. (There were religious Zionists, in what was called the **Mizrahi** movement, but their numbers were relatively small.) To organize the Yishuv's economy and society, the movement's principal organizational form became that of a labor union—the **Histadrut**, founded in 1920. Within the Histadrut, sections were formed devoted to particular tasks. One of these, which constructed buildings and roads, was called *Solel Boneh*.

Before long it became clear that, because of Arab opposition and violence, the Yishuv would need some sort of paramilitary defense and police organization. It formed this force, called the **Haganah**, in 1920.

It was also necessary for the Zionists, who came from diverse lands, to speak a common language. The obvious choice was Hebrew, but that tongue had not been in use as an everyday spoken language for more than 1,000 years. Eliezer Ben-Yehuda undertook the task of writing a dictionary and creating a modernized grammar for Hebrew, after which the members of the movement dedicated themselves to learning and speaking modern Hebrew—even though none of them spoke Hebrew as their first language. This willing into being of a modern language, and the voluntary adaptation of it by an entire community, is an event unique in modern history. (Other languages have been deliberately modernized, Hungarian being a good example; but the vast majority of Hungarians started out speaking Hungarian as their first language.) The movement founded a university in Jerusalem, also in 1920, to emphasize the rebirth of Hebrew culture; it was called, logically enough, the Hebrew University. (It remains the most prestigious university in Israel, though it has since been joined by Tel Aviv University, Haifa University, and Ben-Gurion University.)

Each of the main factions of the Zionist movement focused on building up the agricultural sector. Much of their energy went into the **kibbutz** movement. A kibbutz is a collective farm, where everything is owned in common. All profit from sales is pooled, and committees apportion work and make all investment and management decisions. Most early kibbutzim also believed in the creation of a new social order; while traditional institutions like marriage were tolerated, they were not obligatory. Children did not live in the same

A photograph of Kibbutz Dan, which is located in the Upper Galilee near Kiryat Shemona. The first kibbutz, or collective farm, was started in Palestine around 1910; today, there are about 270 kibbutzim in Israel.

buildings with their parents, but rather in children's houses, where members of the kibbutz took turns caring for them. The kibbutz movement was to agriculture what the Histadrut was to industry.

Socialist Zionism was not a religious but a national movement. In fact, most socialist Zionists were actually anti-religious. There were no synagogues on socialist kibbutzim, and the traditional Jewish holidays were either ignored or changed into secular, nationalist celebrations. But the socialist-minded leadership understood that most potential immigrants to Palestine were not socialist ideologues, but more traditionally minded people. Therefore, the movement did not reject the Jewish heritage, but tried to modernize it. (So, for example, it was decided that the Yishuv should use the Jewish calendar in parallel to the general "Christian" one.) An arrangement was made between the secular and religious wings of the movement in which the Orthodox Rabbinate was given responsibility for and authority over the religious institutions of the country. So the Yishuv had a chief rabbi, the most famous and important of whom was Avraham Yitzhak Kook.

All of these institutions—the Zionist Executive, the Jewish National Fund, the World Zionist Organization, the Histadrut, the Haganah, the kibbutz movement, and so on—grew and matured in the 1920s, 1930s, and early 1940s.

During the 1930s many Jews immigrated to Palestine from central and eastern European countries such as Poland, Hungary, and Romania in order to escape collapsing economies and rising anti-Semitism. In certain respects the majority of these people differed from the socialist Zionists who had been building Jewish institutions in Palestine. For one thing, most did not share an affinity with socialist ideology. In addition, they tended to be urban dwellers, and they were not interested in kibbutzim. These immigrants founded a non-socialist political movement, known as

Yitzhak Rabin, in a 1976 photograph. Rabin (1922–1995) served as a leader of the elite Palmach force, which raided Arab strongholds in Syria and Lebanon in the 1940s. Rabin eventually became a general in the Israeli army, and served as Israel's prime minister twice (1974–77 and 1992–95). He shared the 1994 Nobel Peace Prize with Palestinian leader Yasir Arafat and Israeli foreign minister Shimon Peres for their work in negotiating a peace settlement to end the violence in the Middle East. He also negotiated a 1994 peace treaty with Jordan, which became the second Arab country to recognize Israel. On November 4, 1995, Rabin was assassinated after attending a rally in Tel Aviv.

Revisionist Zionism. Its most important leader during the Yishuv period was the Russian-born Vladimir Jabotinsky.

Almost none of the leaders of the Zionist movement came from democratic countries. But because of the diversity of the movement's members, the admiration of many of its leaders for Britain and the United States, and the different ideological schools within the movement, Zionism developed a democratic ethos. Weizmann and Ben-Gurion also had personal leadership styles that accentuated democratic decision-making.

During the 1930s, as Arab violence against Jews increased and as British Mandate authorities sought to appease Palestinian Arabs, some Zionists, especially among the Revisionists, began to advocate expelling the British from Palestine by force. They also decided to answer Arab violence with violence of their own. They formed paramilitary organizations separate from the Haganah, including the ***Irgun*** and the even more radical Stern Gang. (Two members of the Irgun at this time, Menachem Begin and Yitzhak Shamir, would both later become Israeli prime ministers.) Mainstream Zionists for the most part opposed violence against the British and all opposed violence against innocent Arabs. They did, however, create an elite force within the Haganah to protect the Yishuv and to engage in other special operations. This was called the **_Palmach_**, and one of its members was Yitzhak Rabin, who later became a general in the Israeli army and twice served as prime minister.

The Economy of Israel

Gross domestic product (GDP*): $119 billion (purchasing power parity)

GDP per capita: $20,000 (purchasing power parity)

Inflation: 1.1%

Natural resources: timber, potash, copper ore, natural gas, phosphate rock, magnesium bromide, clays, sand

Agriculture (4% of GDP): citrus fruits, vegetables, cotton; beef, poultry, dairy products (1999 est.)

Industry (37% of GDP): high-technology projects (including aviation, communications, computer-aided design and manufactures, medical electronics), wood and paper products, potash and phosphates, food, beverages, tobacco, caustic soda, cement, diamond cutting (1999 est.)

Services (59% of GDP): government services, banking, tourism (1999 est.)

Foreign trade:

Imports—$30.6 billion: raw materials, military equipment, fuels, raw diamonds, consumer goods.

Exports—$26.5 billion: machinery, software, cut diamonds, agricultural products, chemicals, textiles, apparel.

Currency exchange rate: 4.8380 Israeli shekels = U.S. $1 (January 2003)

*GDP, or gross domestic product, is the total value of goods and services produced in a country annually.
All figures are 2001 estimates unless otherwise noted.
Sources: CIA World Factbook, 2002; Bloomberg.com.

INSTITUTIONS IN THE STATE OF ISRAEL

After independence was proclaimed in May 1948, the institutions of the Yishuv essentially became the institutions of the new State of Israel. The Histadrut became, in essence, the economic planning center of the society. The Haganah became the army, the Israel Defense Forces (***Tzahal***, for short, in the Hebrew acronym); it furnished most of the leaders for the new ministry of defense. The Chief Rabbinate of the Jewish community during the Mandate period became the Chief Rabbinate of the State of Israel. The new ministry of agriculture became, for the most part, an organizational mechanism for the kibbutz movement. Solel Boneh became part of the ministry of housing and infrastructure. Many who had been active within the Yishuv as representatives to the World Zionist Organization became members of the new ministries of foreign affairs and absorption. The leaders of the Zionist Executive became the leaders of the new government, and the Zionist Executive itself was transformed into a government with an executive, legislative, and judicial branch.

Israel also set up municipal governments, but since the country is so small, the national government tended to have control over most functions. Only the mayors of Israel's largest cities—Jerusalem, Tel Aviv, Haifa, and Beersheba—have had very important and difficult jobs.

The executive branch became the prime ministry, with Ben-Gurion serving as the nation's first prime minister. (Israel also created a position of president, but it was largely ceremonial in design. The position was first offered to Albert Einstein, who had long been a supporter of Zionism, but Einstein declined—so an aged Chaim Weizmann became Israel's first president.)

Israel's legislative branch consists of a parliament called the ***Knesset*** (which means "assembly"). Under Israel's parliamentary

The Knesset, Israel's parliament, meets in this building in Jerusalem. The 120-member Knesset makes laws and elects the president of Israel. Members of the Knesset are elected every four years.

system—which was modeled basically upon that of Great Britain—the voters select not individuals but parties. Each party presents a list of candidates, and the better the party does in the election, the more members of its list win seats in the parliament. The number one person on the list of the most successful party becomes prime minister. If no single party wins a majority of the seats in parliament—as is generally the case—the leading party must form a governing coalition with other parties, whose leaders will receive ministerial posts in exchange for their support.

Israel's judicial system was also modeled largely on the British system, but the Israeli High Court also has some features in common with the U.S. Supreme Court. In addition, Israel set up religious courts to handle ritual and most life-cycle matters. These are not just Jewish; there are such courts for Muslims and Christians as well. In Israel, for example, it was not possible (and still isn't possible) to get married by a justice of the peace. All marriages have to be officiated by clergy.

Israel held its first election in 1949, and the socialist Zionist labor parties (there were three main ones, called Mapai, Mapam, and Achdut Ha-avodah) won most of the seats. They formed a government with some religious parties.

One reason for this was that the leaders of the Zionist movement, and now the new State of Israel, could not decide how to write a constitution for the country. The main problem was how to reconcile disagreements over the relationship between Judaism and the Jewish state. Religious Zionists wanted Jewish religious law, called **halacha**, to become binding in Israel. But the secular leaders of the movement disagreed. They wanted all citizens to have equal rights regardless of whether they were Jews. The Arabs who remained in Israel after the 1948 War of Independence became full citizens of the state, with full legal rights. If Israel were a state formally tied up with Judaism as a religion, this would scarcely be possible.

Informally, the socialist leaders agreed to let the Orthodox Rabbinate continue the relationship established in the Mandate period, but they refused to acknowledge any explicitly religious basis for the state. In Israel's 1948 Declaration of Independence, the movement could not even agree on whether to mention God. A compromise was reached; the declaration speaks of "the rock of Israel," and since Hebrew has no capital letters, those who want "rock" to mean God can think that, and those who want it to stand for something else can think that. In any event, the result is that Israel was set up as a Jewish state, but not one in which Judaism as such has special legal status. As far as Israel's pro-secularist founders were concerned, Jewish civilization is larger than Judaism as a religion, and a modern civilization would not, or at any rate should not, be ruled by or bound by religion or religious law as such. As far as

The United States was the first country to officially recognize the State of Israel. This is a draft copy of President Harry S. Truman's remarks, which he made the evening of May 14, 1948—11 minutes after the British mandate for Palestine officially expired.

Israel's religious Zionists were concerned, Judaism and Jewish religious law define Jewish civilization, and hence ought to define its political expression: the state. In 1948–49, a compromise was worked out: the state would let the rabbis run Jewish communal affairs on the basis of Jewish law, and the rabbis would let the secular Zionist leaders rule the country. It was on the basis of this agreement that Israel's first government was formed.

This basic disagreement has never been settled, and Israel, therefore, still has no constitution. It operates according to a series of Basic Laws, passed by the Knesset, that have a higher status than regular laws. There were eight of these laws until the 1990s, when three more were added. Some Israelis today want to see a constitution written, but others, who point out that Great Britain does not have a constitution either, are not so inclined.

Mourners weep as the bodies of slain Israelis arrive at Tel Aviv Airport, September 1972. During the 1972 Summer Olympics, Arab terrorists killed 11 Israeli athletes and coaches. Terrorism has been a constant problem since the foundation of the State of Israel in 1948.

Society, Politics, and Foreign Policy, 1949–1977

J srael began its life as an independent country with clear goals. Basically these goals were to provide a haven for Jews all over the world, to rebuild the pride as well as the security of the Jewish people in the wake of the Holocaust, to develop Jewish culture in all forms, and to reconnect the Jewish people to their own history in their own land. The country's national anthem, "HaTikvah" ("The Hope"), speaks of the Jewish people never having lost hope for 2,000 years in their restoration to Zion (the Jewish homeland).

Despite its citizens' high morale and its clear national goals, though, Israel in its infancy faced serious problems. The main ones, basically, were that Israel was small and hated by all of its much more populous immediate neighbors, and that it had a significant Arab minority whose attitudes toward the state were not known. Building a strong society and a viable economy from refugees who, despite their common Jewish roots, came from dozens of different countries was no easy task either. In addition, despite its considerable human talent, Israel has few valuable natural resources, aside from some minerals mainly around the Dead Sea; there is no oil or gas, and only 17 percent of the land is arable.

POPULATION GROWTH

Despite these problems, Israel thrived in its first dozen years. By the end of 1949, there were about 880,000 people in Israel, of whom about 717,000 were Jews (more Arabs left Israel after the armistice agreements). By 1961, there were 2.18 million people, of whom 1.93 million were Jews. The more than doubling of the population in such a short period of time was attributable to a very large absorption of immigrants, as well as a high rate of natural increase. By 1972 Israel's population reached 3.15 million, of whom 2.69 million were Jews.

This rapid rate of population growth had many effects. First, it showed Israelis and others that Israel was a viable state and society and was here to stay. The more people there were in the country, the larger and more widespread their physical presence in the land could be. Second, the population increase enabled very striking economic growth in absolute terms, for more people means more workers and more consumption, and thus a larger economy. Third, Israel's population growth made it a much more diverse society, and this is of particular and long-lasting importance.

Many of the immigrants in Israel's first two decades came from Arab and other non-Western countries. Jews had lived in places like Egypt, Morocco, Algeria, Yemen, Iran, Syria, and Libya for many centuries. When Israel was established, the status of these Jews in their countries of residence changed. While they had always been second-class citizens, they were rarely harmed physically. But Arab resentment of Israel led some Arab governments to encourage harassment and violence against the Jews. Also, many Jews in these countries were traditionally religious people, and many interpreted the establishment of the State of Israel as the dawn of their redemption, so they wished to return to Zion. In some cases, too—particularly in the case of the large population of Iraqi Jews—Israeli officials actively sought to persuade the community to immigrate to Israel. Whatever the reasons, very large numbers of Jews from these countries came to Israel. These people were not European in culture, as the founders of the Zionist movement and most of the Yishuv had been. Most did not speak any European language (though many from North Africa spoke French), and they did not have the kind of technical education that European-oriented Jews in Israel had. Some, such as most of those from Yemen, had

Israel today is a mixture of people from all over the world. Jews make up slightly more than 80 percent of the country's 6 million people. Jews from Europe or America make up about 32 percent of the total population, with native-born Israelis at nearly 21 percent, Jews from Africa (mostly northern Africa, South Africa, and Ethiopia) at just under 15 percent, and Jews from Asia at about 13 percent. The remaining one-fifth of the population is mostly Arab.

The People of Israel

Population: 6,029,520 (July 2002 est.)
Ethnic groups: Jewish, 80.1%; Arab, 18.1%; other, 1.8% (1996 est.)
Religions: Jewish, 80.1%; Muslim (mostly Sunni), 14.6%; Christian, 2.1%; other, 3.2% (1996 est.)
Languages: Hebrew (official); Arabic used officially for Arab minority; English most commonly used foreign language
Age structure:
   0–14 years: 27.1%
   15–64 years: 63%
   65 years and over: 9.9%
Population growth rate: 1.48%
Birth rate: 18.91 births/1,000 population
Death rate: 6.21 deaths/1,000 population
Infant mortality rate: 7.55 deaths/1,000 live births
Life expectancy at birth:
   total population: 78.76 years
   males: 81.01 years
   females: 76.82 years
Total fertility rate: 2.54 children born/woman
Literacy (age 15 and older): 95% (1992 est.)

All figures are 2002 estimates unless otherwise noted.
Source: CIA World Factbook, 2002.

never seen running water or electricity before coming to Israel. Most, though not all, were poor and so could not finance their own resettlement. Hence, their absorption was a great economic challenge.

But it was accomplished. In 1948 there were 591,400 Jews in Israel of European origin—called ***Ashkenazim***, after the Hebrew word for Germany. There were only 105,000 from non-European cultures—called ***Sephardim***, after the Hebrew word for Spain. (This was an unfortunate choice of words, because Jews who used to live in Spain and Portugal before they were expelled in 1492 had their own special traditions and language, called Ladino, and these differed as much from Yemenite or Iraqi Jewish traditions as they did from those of Germany or Poland. Some therefore prefer the term *Oriental Jews* to refer to those who came to Israel from non-Western countries, the term simply meaning from the East instead of the West. Most Israelis came to refer to these people as being from the

Most residents of Israel live in the northern part of the country; the Negev Desert to the south is only sparsely inhabited.

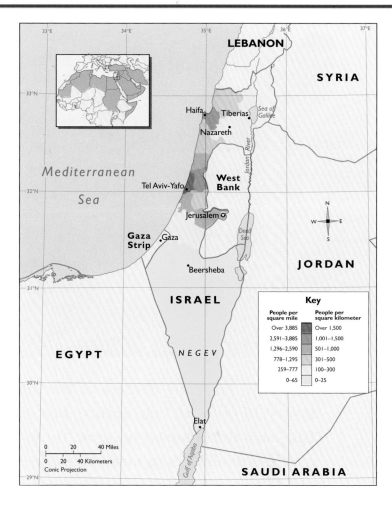

Edot Misrakhit, the "eastern communities.") But by 1961 there were 1.01 million Ashkenazim and 818,330 Sephardim. By 1972 the balance had shifted: there were 1.19 million Ashkenazim and 1.27 million Sephardim. Of course, as time passed, a higher percentage of Jews in Israel were born there instead of having come as immigrants. Those Jews born in Israel came to be known as *sabras*, after the cactus that grows wild in the land.

There were social problems between the ruling Ashkenazi elite and the Sephardic newcomers. Some of the elite looked down on the newcomers; some of the newcomers resented the power of the elite and the way they were initially treated. Many of the newcomers were

Israeli troops train in the desert, 1956. Even today nearly all Israelis serve in the army; men are required to enlist for three years, while women serve for two years. Military service is not compulsory for Israeli Arabs and ultra-Orthodox Jewish students.

settled in far-flung corners of the state, in so-called development towns, in order to help secure the land and broaden the economy. But for natural social reasons, these towns tended to be shabbier and less wealthy than more established towns, and their educational systems and social-service networks were not as good. Even today there is still some resentment between the groups, but not nearly as much. One reason is that Israel is a kind of pressure cooker in which everyone undergoes similar socializing experiences. One of the most important of these is obligatory military service.

MILITARY AND SECURITY ISSUES

Almost every Israeli Jew, male and female, enters the army after finishing high school at age 18. (Israeli Arabs can join, but they are not required to do so.) Army life has been a homogenizing agent in Israeli society. It was particularly important in Israel's early years as an independent country, for it was the main method of creating a common cultural experience for all people. It was how newcomers learned fluent spoken Hebrew, how they learned to bond with others outside of their culture of origin, and how they learned about the country physically as they traveled about on exercises and deployments. Many people also met their future spouses in the army, and this greatly speeded up intermarriage rates between Ashkenazim and Sephardim.

Initially, the Arab citizens of Israel were placed under special security rule, which did not technically end until 1966. But it soon became fairly clear that they posed little or no security threat. They were rarely responsible for violence or sabotage of any kind. They never engaged in terrorism. Many came to appreciate the benefits that living in Israel brought them: a thriving economy, better schools, and democracy. From the very first election, Arabs voted, formed their own parties, and elected members to the Knesset. From 1949 on, there have always been Arab members of the Knesset. But between 1949 and 1977, no Israeli Arab served as a cabinet member, though there were a few Arabs in Israel's diplomatic service.

Although Arabs living within Israel did not present a security risk, Arabs living outside the country did. Palestinians from Gaza (which was under Egyptian control after the 1948–49 war) and Palestinians from Jordan infiltrated Israel and committed acts of terrorism. During the 1950s Israelis lived in constant fear of terrorist incursions; between 1951 and 1956 more than 400 people were murdered and 900 injured in such incidents. On a few occasions, the Israeli army launched raids in Gaza and Jordan's West Bank to punish terrorists and to force the governments, especially in Jordan, to exert more control over their borders. Israelis still debate whether these incursions did more good or more harm.

During the first years of its existence as an independent state, Israel's relations with its Arab neighbors remained tense. Between 1949 and 1956, the Arab states—which had formed an organization called the Arab League to pursue their common interests—continued to reject Israel's right to exist. Though defeated in battle, they refused to make peace, and their propaganda spoke constantly about the "next battle" that would destroy Israel and push the Jews into the sea. Still, there were no major battles between Israel and its Arab neighbors during this period. There were, however, a few skirmishes between the Israeli and Syrian armies near Lake Tiberias, around demilitarized zones established in 1948–49 that did not exactly match the international boundaries there. Some of these skirmishes involved Israel's effort to divert the Jordan River waters into its National Water Carrier—an extensive system of irrigation pipes that would bring water to Israel's coastal plain and to the Negev Desert for agricultural expansion. The Arabs wanted to

stop this plan because they believed it would strengthen Israel. They also claimed that Israel was stealing water that was theirs, even though according to international law this was not true. Israel managed to complete the National Water Carrier, which began full operation in 1964. But thereafter, the Arab countries planned to divert one of the main sources of the Jordan River before it flowed into Israel; Israel responded by bombing the diversion works in Syria.

An aerial view of a canal in northern Israel. This canal is part of the National Water Carrier system, which brings water to the coastal plain and the Negev Desert.

THE SUEZ CRISIS AND THE SINAI CAMPAIGN

In 1952 a group of Egyptian army commanders known as the Free Officers overthrew Egypt's king and took control of the government. The leader of the Free Officers, a colonel named Gamal Abdel Nasser, had dreams of uniting the Arab world, and he was virulently anti-Israel. Within a few years, Nasser's actions, set against the backdrop of the **Cold War**, drew Israel—along with France and Great Britain—into a military conflict with his country.

Seeking to increase its influence in the Arab world—and to contain its Cold War enemy, the communist Soviet Union—the United States agreed to finance a major development project, the Aswan Dam, in Egypt. At the same time, however, Nasser courted the Soviets—who were only too happy to gain a foothold in strategic Egypt—and pursued his anti-Israel agenda. A series of escalating terror raids launched against Israel from Gaza prompted Prime Minister David Ben-Gurion in 1955 to order an Israeli strike in Gaza. The Israeli army easily overran the Egyptian positions, with the Egyptian defenders beating a hasty retreat. Concerned by his troops' poor performance, Nasser sought to buy military equipment to strengthen the Egyptian armed forces. Because the U.S. administration of President Dwight Eisenhower refused to sell arms to Egypt, Nasser turned to the Soviet Union, which agreed to supply a large quantity of weapons, including aircraft and tanks, through the Soviet-controlled communist country of Czechoslovakia.

This development particularly concerned Israel, which pleaded with the United States for a defense pact. Israeli officials argued that unless the United States promised to protect their nation, Israel might have to act on its own or with others to deal with the Egyptian threat before it was too late. The United States refused, fearing that military or defense support for Israel would enable the Soviet Union to gain additional influence over the Arabs and jeopardize Western-

Military leader Moshe Dayan (1915–1981) was a hero of Israel's 1956 Sinai Campaign against Egypt; he later served as Israel's defense minister and minister of foreign affairs. While serving in the latter post, Dayan helped to negotiate the 1978 peace agreement between Israel and Egypt.

held oil concessions in the Arab countries. (That is why, before the 1967 war, Israel got its weapons not from the United States, but mainly from France and other European countries.)

Events in 1956 drew Israel, France, and Britain together to oppose Egyptian threats to their interests. In that year, amid growing communist influence in Egypt, the Eisenhower administration decided to withdraw U.S. financing for the Aswan Dam project—a potentially severe blow to Egypt's economic prospects. Nasser responded by *nationalizing* the Suez Canal, which, though it runs through Egyptian territory, was operated by a company with British and French shareholders. Britain and France were worried that Nasser might close the canal to their ships and thereby cut off a vital trade route. For its part, Israel worried about the continuing threat from Egypt; in addition to the vitriolic rhetoric and violent incursions from Gaza, Nasser had cut off Israel's access to the Red Sea by blockading the Strait of Tiran at the southern end of the Gulf of Aqaba. So Israel, Britain, and France colluded in a plan to roll back the Egyptian military, secure the Suez Canal—and drive Nasser from power.

On October 29, 1956, Israel invaded Egypt's Sinai Peninsula. Two days later, British and French forces—invoking a 1950 treaty that authorized them to protect the Suez Canal—struck near the northern (Mediterranean) entrance to the canal.

The Sinai Campaign, as the Israelis came to call their military action, went remarkably well. Under the leadership of Chief of Staff Moshe Dayan, Israeli units quickly overwhelmed Egyptian forces in the Sinai and pushed toward the eastern bank of the Suez Canal. Meanwhile, the British and French forces managed to occupy the strategic Egyptian city of Port Said, at the northern end of the canal, and pushed to within about 25 miles (40 km) of Suez City, near the southern end. But the British and French operation was delayed and awkward, and it did not push Nasser from power. Then the realities of superpower politics and the Cold War began to play into the war in unexpected ways. The Soviet Union condemned the invasion of Egypt and threatened to send troops to the Suez, and even to strike France and Great Britain directly. Surprisingly, however, the United States also strongly opposed the invasion. Worried that U.S. acquiescence in the attack on Egypt might drive the Arabs into the arms of the Soviet Union, President Eisenhower and Secretary of State John Foster Dulles demanded that Great Britain and France withdraw from the Suez, and that Israel withdraw from the Sinai.

After about six months of negotiations, Israel withdrew from the Sinai. In return, it received a promise from the United States and other major countries that the Strait of Tiran would be open to Israeli and Israel-bound shipping, thus allowing the port city of

Eilat to prosper, and that UN peacekeeping troops would be stationed on the Sinai Peninsula to provide a buffer with Egypt.

In the aftermath of the Suez Crisis, as the incident was called in the West, the United States still refused to sell weapons to Israel or to sign a security pact with it. Instead, the United States worked in secret with the British government to find ways to solve the Arab-Israeli conflict. The Israeli government thought territorial concessions near Lake Tiberias and in the Negev Desert, which the U.S. administration wanted Israel to agree to, were dangerous and unreasonable. For their part, the Arabs rejected the U.S. proposals because in the end they would require the Arab nations to recognize and make peace with Israel.

FOREIGN RELATIONS TO 1967

Until 1967 Israel's closest allies were France, Britain, and other European countries. The Federal Republic of Germany in particular established special ties with Israel in recognition of Nazi Germany's terrible guilt in perpetrating the Holocaust against the Jews. Germany agreed to pay the Israeli government and many individual Israeli citizens reparations for damage done during World War II, and Germany quietly sold Israel small arms and other military equipment. Israel used German reparation payments, money raised from Jews in the United States and elsewhere, and foreign aid from the United States to help absorb new immigrants and build a strong society and economy. Israel's close relationship with West European governments was also fostered by a shared democratic socialist philosophy.

Israel's relations with the United States, though generally good, were periodically strained by diplomatic tensions. Its relations with the Soviet Union and the other communist countries were poor, particularly as anti-Semitic attitudes grew stronger in the Soviet Union and in the Eastern bloc generally.

Israel also developed friendly relations with many newly independent African countries in the late 1950s and early 1960s. Many African leaders saw Israel as a model of success in how national liberation movements could build up their countries. Many African students went to Israel to study in Israeli universities, and Israel sent economic and technical aid teams, especially for agriculture, to help African countries develop their economies. Israel also established security cooperation and good relations with non-Arab countries on the periphery of the Arab world, especially Iran, Ethiopia, and Turkey. Israel also worked to establish close ties with the world's most populous democracy, India, but the Indian government took a pro-Arab position to make it hard for its adversary, Muslim Pakistan, to monopolize Arab support in the Indo-Pakistani conflict.

ARAB RIVALRIES AND THE PLO

In 1964 the Palestine Liberation Organization (PLO) was formed, in Cairo under Egyptian sponsorship. The organization was formed to coordinate and focus the Palestinian "national revolution"—the armed struggle to "liberate" what they saw as their homeland, which was defined as all the territory included in British Mandate Palestine. In theory, while the Arab states were united behind this goal, the Palestinians would direct their own national movement. As Article 28 of the PLO's covenant states, "The Palestinian Arab people insists upon the originality and independence of its national revolution, and rejects every manner of interference, trusteeship and subordination."

In reality, Arab politics played a not insignificant role in the formation of the PLO and the subsequent course of the Palestinian "revolution." As some observers have noted, the PLO was conceived largely as a way to bring the Palestinian movement under the control of Arab governments. At the same time, Arab leaders could point to their support for the PLO as evidence of their solidarity with the displaced Palestinians, thereby increasing their prestige within the Arab world. Egypt's president, Gamal Abdel Nasser, was making a bid to unify the Arab world (or as much of it as he could) under Egyptian leadership. But other Arab regimes in Iraq, Syria, Saudi Arabia, and Jordan also aspired to more influence and power. This competition was called the Arab Cold War.

In February 1966 a coup in Syria brought to power a radical Arab nationalist government. Not wanting to be outdone by Egypt, the new Syrian regime developed its own Palestinian group. In Kuwait it found an Egyptian-born Palestinian named Yasir Arafat and his small, weak, and previously obscure organization, called Fatah. With support from Syria, Fatah commandos carried out terror raids inside Israel. In one of these raids, Fatah terrorists attacked a school bus, killing dozens of Israeli children. Meanwhile, the Egyptian-backed PLO had hardly ever carried out any successful raids against Israel.

An escalated competition ensued between Egypt's Palestinians and Syria's Palestinians, and between the Egyptian and Syrian governments. But this competition among Arabs mainly harmed Israelis, as the level and frequency of terrorist attacks rose. During this period, the Soviet Union was arming both Egypt and Syria, and encouraging attacks against Israel. Not only did this enhance Moscow's prestige in Arab eyes, it also put pressure on the United States, which at the time was bogged down in the Vietnam War.

THE SIX-DAY WAR AND ITS AFTERMATH

But Nasser eventually overplayed his hand. In May 1967 he announced that the Strait of Tiran was closed to Israeli-bound shipping, which violated the promises made to Israel in 1956–57 and was technically an act of war. He also ordered the United Nations buffer force put in the Sinai after 1956 to leave, and to nearly everyone's surprise it did. Nasser probably did not want a war. His best soldiers were fighting in a civil war in Yemen against forces backed by Saudi Arabia, and in previous years he had said many times that Egypt could not afford, and probably could not win, a war against Israel.

But war fever spread in the Arab world. Pro-war and pro-Nasser riots broke out among Palestinians in the West Bank, and to restore order the Jordanian army was called in and martial law proclaimed. Iraqi forces insisted on transiting Jordanian territory to get to Israel, and Jordan's King Hussein had no choice but to let them. Before long, King Hussein joined Egypt in a war party, fearing that he would be overthrown from within otherwise. With this, Nasser lost control of the ploy he had set in motion, whose original aim had probably only been to reverse the one gain Israel had gotten from the Sinai Campaign: the opening of the port city of Eilat to international maritime traffic.

As all this was happening, an alarmed Israel turned to the United States for help. Israel asked the United States to make good on its pledge to keep the Strait of Tiran open to Israel, by leading an international naval armada to break the Egyptian blockade. The United States, under President Lyndon Johnson, did not act.

Meanwhile, Israel had mobilized its entire society to prepare for war, which meant mobilizing its vast reserve system, which in turn effectively shut down the economy. Israel could not maintain such a mobilization for very long. With Arab rhetoric growing shriller every day, with no help coming from the United States, and with Arab armies marching toward Israel from as far away as Iraq and Morocco, Israel decided to act first to defuse the threat.

On June 5, Israeli warplanes attacked air bases in Egypt and Syria. Caught off guard, the Arab air forces were almost completely destroyed on the ground. Israel informed Jordanian leaders—with whom Israeli officials had maintained a secret dialogue since

1964—that if Jordan did not attack Israel, Israel would not attack Jordan. But King Hussein had put his army under Egyptian command, and it did attack Israel.

In just six days of fighting, the Israeli military, led by its chief of staff, Yitzhak Rabin, routed the combined forces of Jordan, Syria, and Egypt. By the time Syria accepted a cease-fire on June 10 to end the war, Israel occupied the West Bank, Syria's Golan Heights, and, once again, Gaza and Egypt's Sinai Peninsula. Israel had also taken the Old City of Jerusalem, which contains the holiest sites to the Jewish people—including the Wailing Wall, the last remnant of the Second Temple destroyed by the Romans in the year 70.

Israelis were both relieved and jubilant in the aftermath of the Six-Day War, as the conflict came to be called. The Arabs, on the other hand, were humiliated; except for Jordanian troops fighting in Jerusalem, Israel had completely rolled over the Arab forces. The Egyptian army crumbled before the Israeli onslaught; many of its soldiers threw down their weapons and tried to run away. Israeli forces could have marched all the way to Cairo and Damascus had they wished.

Israel's stunning military victory led to political and strategic complications that have proved exceedingly difficult to sort out even to this day. Perhaps the most intractable problem involved the West Bank. Although the Six-Day War—like Israel's War of Independence two decades earlier—produced tens of thousands of Palestinian refugees, in 1967 the majority of West Bank Palestinians did not leave their homes. Thus Israel found itself in control of a territory whose population was largely hostile to the Israeli occupation—and even, in certain quarters, to the very idea of Israel's existence. Over the long term, this situation became a recipe for bloodshed.

Initially, however, the Israeli government believed that it would be able to trade the territories it occupied in the 1967 war for peace treaties with the Arab states. Indeed, this is the offer Israel made after the war. American and French intermediaries conveyed to the Arab states Israel's willingness to give back most, though not all, of the West Bank to Jordan; nearly all of the Golan Heights to Syria; and all of Sinai to Egypt. To Israel's surprise and dismay, the Arab states refused the offer. Instead, at a meeting of Arab heads of state in Khartoum, Sudan, in November 1967, they proclaimed what became known as the Three No's: no recognition of Israel, no nego-

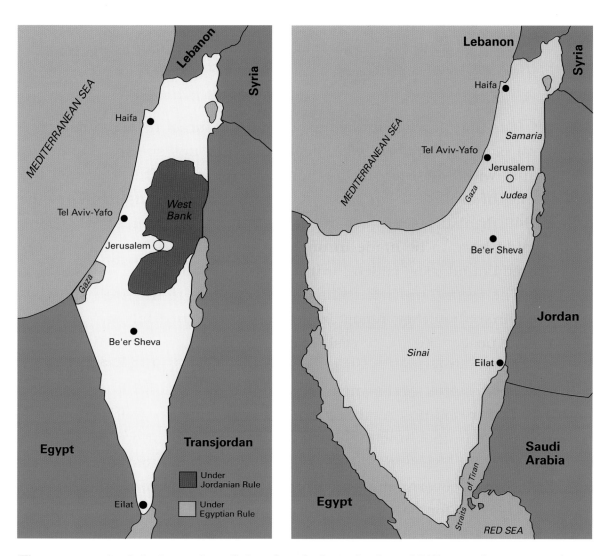

The map on the left shows Israel's borders before the June 1967 war; the map on the right, the territory under Israeli control after the fighting ended.

tiations, and no peace.

That same month, the United Nations Security Council passed Resolution 242, which became the basis for all international diplomacy aiming at peace between Israel and its neighbors. The core of the resolution was contained in the following two provisions:

(i) Withdrawal of Israeli armed forces from territories occupied in the recent conflict;

(ii) Termination of all claims or states of belligerency and respect for and acknowledgement of the sovereignty, territorial integrity and political independence of every State in the area and their right to live in peace within secure and recognized boundaries free from threats or acts of force.

The first provision, obviously, required Israel to relinquish control of occupied land. Significantly, it did not specify that Israel must withdraw from *all* territories it occupied. This reflected the belief of most of the representatives that some adjustments to the 1949 armistice lines separating Israel from Jordan's West Bank would have to be made in order to create the "secure and recognized boundaries" called for in the second provision.

The second provision was directed mainly to the Arab states. It required that they recognize Israel's right to exist and formally make peace with the Jewish state.

Although Israel stated its willingness to accept Resolution 242, the Arab states, and some other countries as well, took the position that the resolution required Israel to withdraw from all territories it occupied in the June 1967 war *before* any negotiations over secure borders for Israel could proceed. For their part, most Israelis—and the Israeli government—advocated trading some of the land taken in the war for peace if that was possible. But no one proposed returning the Old City of Jerusalem, now Israel's united capital, to Jordan. In addition, some of the heirs of the Revisionist Zionists from the Mandate period, represented in the opposition parties in the Knesset called Herut and Gahal, wanted to keep the West Bank and most if not all of the Golan Heights. Some of Israel's religious parties, too, which had been political allies of the dominant Labor Party since 1949, agreed that these territories were part of the Jewish Promised Land and should not be returned. The Revisionists argued that since the Arabs had caused the war and now refused to make peace, they did not deserve to have their land back. The religious parties took a theological, not a political or strategic, view, but they now had more in common with the Revisionist Zionists than ever before.

The Six-Day War contributed to an increase in religiosity in a society composed largely of secular Jews. Among religious Jews, members of the group referred to as modern Orthodox tend to be very nationalistic, fusing nationalist and religious ideas into support for Greater Israel—meaning Israel defined as the original country plus the occupied territories. Another group of religious Israeli Jews, called *haredim*, or "ultra-Orthodox," are traditionally non-Zionist—they do not believe in the legitimacy of the Jewish state, for they think that only God, when He sends the Messiah, can rebuild the state. The ***haredim***, who wear distinctive, usually black clothing and often continue to speak Yiddish instead of Hebrew among themselves, live in Israel for religious rather than political reasons. Hence they try not to serve in the army or other institutions of the state. They do, however, have political parties and try to influence government policy in their favor. They also have separate school systems and, unlike modern Orthodox Jews, live apart from other Israelis. Even among this non-Zionist group, the 1967 war produced a certain nationalistic fervor; the *haredim* wanted Israel to maintain control over the occupied territories. In general, a kind of national triumphalism after 1967 led to an increase in both religious devotion and nationalism—including, very importantly, among the Sephardim in Israel.

But it would be incorrect to suggest that Israeli society remained politically united in the aftermath of the Six-Day War. For example, many secular and modern Orthodox Israelis came increasingly to resent the attitudes and power of the *haredi* community, which often seemed to exert a political influence disproportionate to their numbers.

Between 1967 and 1977, the Labor-led Israeli government—which tended to be moderate to left-wing—tried to balance political pressures concerning the occupied territories. Except for Jerusalem, it did not **annex** any of the territories to Israel. But it did sponsor the building of some Jewish settlements in the territories, which served several purposes: to push the Arab states to come to the negotiating table, to relieve pressure from the opposition to settle Jewish patrimonial land, and to appease the powerful kibbutz movement, which was particularly interested in settling the Golan Heights. Most of the settlements built in the decade after the 1967 war were right along the old border—called the Green Line—and around Jerusalem. For security reasons, some were put in the sparsely populated Jordan Valley. No settlements were placed near large Arab towns in the West Bank.

Most of the Israelis who went to live in these settlements did so for economic reasons: the apartments were newer and cheaper than those available inside Israel proper. But some of the settlers were more nationalistic. They were motivated by a patriotic pioneering spirit, similar to, in their minds, the pioneering spirit of the Yishuv. The number of Israelis living in West Bank and Golan Heights settlements as of 1977 was quite small, only about 32,000.

WAR AND PEACE WITH EGYPT

In addition to the changes it brought to Israeli society, the 1967 war had a major effect on the thinking of at least some of the Arab states, and on the Palestinian Arabs in particular. For the first time since Israel's creation, Egypt, Syria, and Jordan had a practical stake in the Arab-Israeli conflict, because their lands were occupied. Before the 1967 war, the interest of the Arab states was mainly political and symbolic.

After the death of Gamal Abdel Nasser in 1970, Anwar Sadat became president of Egypt. In the three years since the Arab defeat in the Six-Day War, the political situation in the Middle East had changed significantly. Particularly with the advent of the Nixon administration in 1969, the United States had developed a much closer security relationship with Israel. Meanwhile France, with whose weapons Israel had won the Six-Day War, suddenly adopted a pro-Arab position, mainly because of oil and commercial concerns. Sadat, who wished to recover the Sinai, realized that to achieve this goal he would have to engage the United States as an intermediary between his nation and Israel. So in the spring of 1972, Sadat suddenly expelled the large Soviet military presence in Egypt, which was a great gain for the United States in the Cold War. In response, Sadat expected the United States to help him start negotiations with Israel, but the Nixon administration was preoccupied with other concerns: getting out of Vietnam, arms control negotiations with the Soviet Union, a major diplomatic opening to China, and the 1972 presidential election.

Frustrated, Sadat took action that was sure to get Washington's attention: he colluded with Syria and Saudi Arabia, and with a Soviet leadership desperate to win back its influence in Egypt, to stage a military demonstration. In 1973, on Yom Kippur, the holiest day of the Jewish year, the Egyptian and Syrian armies launched surprise attacks against Israel, while Saudi Arabia declared an oil embargo against the United States. Most of the world came to call this conflict the October War; Arabs referred to it as the Ramadan War, Israelis as the War of the Day of Judgment.

Israeli forces, taken by surprise, were thrown back and bloodied by the Arab assault. Egyptian soldiers crossed Israel's Bar-Lev line at the Suez Canal, and Syrian forces nearly made their way past the Green Line near Lake Tiberias. For the first time since early 1948, Arab armies were able to inflict real damage on Israeli military forces. Shocked and frightened, the Israelis rallied and fought back. "We will break their bones," declared Israel's defense minister, Moshe Dayan—and that is pretty much what happened. First, the Israeli forces stopped the Syrian advance and pushed the Syrians back beyond the lands taken in 1967. Then, after fighting a holding action in Sinai, they turned to the Egyptian front. The battle in Sinai was the largest armored engagement since World War II. Both sides suffered heavy losses and rapidly depleted their ammunition. The Soviet Union mounted an airborne resupply operation to Egypt, an action that stunned the United States, which was trying to promote better relations between itself and the Soviet Union and

Henry Kissinger, the U.S. secretary of state (left), speaks with Anwar Sadat, president of Egypt. During 1974–75 Kissinger engaged in "shuttle diplomacy," traveling between Israel and both Egypt and Syria to negotiate an end to the October 1973 Arab-Israeli war. He was instrumental in getting the sides to disengage their armies and agree to a truce.

which had only a few months earlier signed a declaration with the Soviet Union forswearing just such behavior. After much hesitation and argument, the Nixon administration undertook a similar resupply operation for Israel—though, because of concerns over Arab oil power, the only U.S. European allies that agreed to help were Portugal and the Netherlands. The 1973 war thus created one of the most dangerous divisions among the Western allies during the entire Cold War.

Having been resupplied by the United States, the Israelis undertook an extremely bold maneuver. Under General Ariel Sharon, they pushed through the Egyptian lines, crossed the Suez Canal into the African side of Egypt, cut off Egyptian supply lines, and encircled the Egyptian army. At this point, the Soviet Union threatened to send Russian soldiers into the battle to stop the Israelis from annihilating the Egyptians. The United States warned the Soviets not to do that and declared a Defense Condition 3 alert level, which basically meant a readiness to fight a nuclear war. Needless to say, tensions were extremely high.

Henry Kissinger, the U.S. secretary of state, believed that a total Israeli victory would not be in anyone's best interests—not even the Israelis'. If its army were crushed, Kissinger recognized, Egypt might be too humiliated to negotiate. So the U.S. government pressured Israel's prime minister, Golda Meir, to agree to a cease-fire.

In the aftermath of the October War and years of U.S.-mediated diplomacy, Sadat launched a bold diplomatic initiative. In November 1977 he traveled to Israel and addressed the Knesset, declaring Egypt's readiness to make peace with Israel. With mediation from the United States, Israel and Egypt ultimately signed a peace treaty, and Israel returned the Sinai to Egypt. U.S. hopes to capitalize on the momentum and broker a peace treaty between Israel and Syria were dashed by the Syrian government's refusal to come to the table. So Israel withdrew from some land in the Golan Heights to disengage the armies, but without a chance to make peace, it held on to the rest.

ISRAEL, JORDAN, AND THE PLO

Before the October War, in 1972, Israel and Jordan had held intense secret negotiations aimed at a peace treaty. But, feeling threatened by more powerful Arab countries, King Hussein of Jordan had been reluctant to compromise. That decision turned out to be costly.

For the Palestinians, the lesson of the 1967 Six-Day War was that the Arab regimes could not be counted on to win back Palestine for them. After 1967 Yasir Arafat's Fatah faction gained control of the Palestine Liberation Organization, and Arafat charted an independent—and bloody—course. The PLO established a virtual state-within-a-state in Jordan, intimidating the local population (and to a certain extent the Jordanian government), launching guerrilla raids into Israel, and carrying out a major terrorist campaign in the Middle East and abroad.

King Hussein's uneasy acceptance of the PLO guerrillas in his midst ended when some of the Palestinian radicals began calling for the overthrow of his regime. In September 1970, the king ordered his army to crush the PLO. In the brief but bloody civil war, the Jordanian troops routed Arafat's forces and faced down a pro-Palestinian invasion from Syria. The PLO was forced to evacuate Jordan almost exactly a year later when Jordanian army troops attacked PLO remnants in the forest of Ajlun—known to Palestinians as "Black September." Thereafter, Palestinian tactics turned to terrorism.

Soon after the fighting in Jordan ended, in 1971, Palestinian terrorists assassinated the Jordanian prime minister, Wasfi al-Tal. In 1972 a PLO group calling itself Black September killed 11 members of the Israeli Olympic team at the Summer Games in Munich, West Germany.

By 1974 the Arab League, over the objections of Jordan, decided that the PLO represented the Palestinian people and that the West Bank belonged to Palestinians (if they could get it back from Israel), not to Jordan. So by not compromising in 1972, King Hussein had ultimately lost an opportunity to get back any of the West Bank—thus reversing his country's gains from the 1948–49 war. By 1974 Jordan was still too weak and vulnerable to make peace with Israel on its own, but Israel and Jordan became tacit allies against radical Palestinian nationalism, which threatened both countries.

Within the framework of Egyptian-Israeli negotiations, Egypt and the United States sought some way of dealing with the Palestinian issue. But the PLO refused to recognize Israel's right to exist in any borders, and Anwar Sadat was unwilling to let Palestinian recalcitrance stand in the way of an Egyptian-Israeli accord—and the return of the Sinai. So the Palestinian issue went unresolved.

THE RISE OF THE LIKUD

By 1977 Israel as an independent state was 28 years old, and during that entire time the Labor Party had led the government. Labor (itself a coalition of other parties) always ruled in coalition with smaller, usually religious, parties. Secular and socialist in basic ideological orientation, the Labor Party was made up of the Ashkenazi elite descended from the main families of the Yishuv leadership—the same elite that also headed up Israel's newspapers, universities, business operations, diplomatic corps, theaters, and kibbutzim. Thus, even though Ashkenazim were no longer a majority among Israel's Jewish population, all the institutions of the state were modeled on Ashkenazi standards and attitudes.

One of the Palestinian Arab terrorists who broke into the Olympic Village in Munich, West Germany, in September 1972, killed two members of the Israeli Olympic team, and took nine others hostage. All the hostages, as well as five terrorists and two Germans (a policeman and a helicopter pilot), were killed during a pitched battle at a Munich airfield.

All of this began to change in May 1977, when Menachem Begin's Herut Party, with its Revisionist allies, beat Labor in national elections and Begin became prime minister. Few people in the United States and Europe knew who Begin was, and fewer still understood his politics and his worldview. They therefore underestimated the extent to which his rise to power would change Israeli policies, just as they failed to comprehend the evolving dynamics of Israeli society that had brought him to power.

Over the years, the Labor Party establishment in Israel had become increasingly ingrown, sclerotic, and corrupt, as any long-tenured political party is liable to get. The Sephardic population, which had grown larger and more involved in politics, organized to gain its share of power. They knew that in Israel's socialist, managed, and patronage-ridden system, they could not get the good jobs unless they had political power. The Labor establishment was not open to their pressures, and so what became known as the Likud opposition (the combination of Herut and Gahal and a few other small factions) took advantage of their discontents. In addition, the religious parties naturally gravitated toward Likud, which also benefited from the nationalist sentiment that had grown after the Six-Day War. Nor had Labor always managed the economy very well. There were periods of high inflation and slow growth, and as Israel's economy grew larger and more sophisticated, many Israelis came to see Labor's socialist-oriented economic policy as wasteful and inefficient. Finally, a minor scandal involving the wife of Labor's leader, Yitzhak Rabin, erupted just before the election, contributing to the party's poor showing.

The Begin government moved quickly to consolidate its control over the Israeli bureaucracy, using the patronage structures created by the Labor elite to put its own people in control and dole out jobs and benefits to its supporters. Though non-socialist in ideology, the new Likud government did not rush to dismantle Israel's patronage system or to privatize government-run businesses. It simply assumed control over them. The real changes in policy were not so much in the domestic arena as in foreign policy and in dealing with the occupied territories.

Menachem Begin and the Likud Party believed that all of the West Bank and most of the Golan Heights were inherently Jewish lands. These territories had been part of the ancient Jewish commonwealths and thus could not be returned to the Arabs. Sinai, on the other hand, was not part of historical **Eretz Yisrael** ("the Land of Israel"), so it had a different status. That is why Begin was able to continue the diplomacy with Egypt that had grown out of the 1973 war.

U.S. president Bill Clinton is flanked by Israeli prime minister Ehud Barak (left) and Palestinian leader Yasir Arafat at the opening of the 2000 Camp David summit. Clinton hoped the summit would provide the final roadmap toward peace and the creation of an autonomous Palestinian state. However, after Arafat rejected the Israeli peace plan, a violent new *intifada* against Israeli targets began.

Society, Politics, and Foreign Policy, 1978-2003

In September 1978, capitalizing on the peace initiative that Anwar Sadat had begun the previous year by visiting Jerusalem, an Israeli-Egyptian summit was held at the U.S. presidential retreat in Camp David, Maryland. Following nearly two weeks of negotiations mediated by President Jimmy Carter, Sadat and Menachem Begin signed an agreement known as the Camp David Accords, which sought to provide a framework for peace in the Middle East. The document committed Israel and Egypt to the goal of concluding a peace treaty within three months; urged other Arab states to negotiate similar peace settlements with Israel; and called on Israel, Egypt, Jordan, and representatives of the Palestinian people to negotiate an acceptable self-government arrangement for the Palestinians of the West Bank and Gaza Strip.

On the matter of Israeli-Egyptian peace, the Camp David Accords succeeded. In March 1979 both countries ratified a peace treaty, and Israel returned the Sinai Peninsula to Egypt in full by April 1982. For Israel, achieving peace with Egypt was a breakthrough of enormous psychological and strategic importance. While relations between Egyptian and Israeli societies were not normalized, the treaty proved that peace between Israel and the Arabs was possible. In addition, by removing the largest and most powerful of the Arab countries from the ranks of Israel's

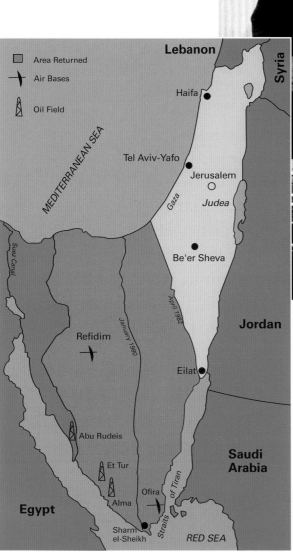

(Top) Egyptian president Anwar Sadat, U.S. president Jimmy Carter, and Israeli prime minister Menachem Begin sign the historic 1979 peace treaty. In the treaty, Israel agreed to return the Sinai Peninsula territory it had occupied since the 1967 war. The map (left) shows the area returned to Egypt. Israel withdrew from the Sinai in two stages. The first withdrawal took place in January 1980 and the second occurred in April 1982.

enemies, it virtually precluded the possibility of another large-scale Arab offensive war against the Jewish state—for without Egypt the Arabs could not hope to prevail militarily.

For Egypt—and Anwar Sadat—peace with Israel came at a price. The Arab League promptly expelled Egypt, and Sadat's domestic situation grew more difficult. In 1981 Islamic extremists assassinated the Egyptian leader.

SETTLEMENTS IN THE WEST BANK

The Camp David Accords did not lead to an overall settlement of the Arab-Israeli conflict, as its architects had hoped. Not only did the other Arab governments fail to follow Sadat's lead, but problems between Israel and the Palestinians gradually got worse.

While Begin was eager for peace with Egypt—and was prepared to give back all of the Sinai to get it—he was opposed to any negotiation that might imperil Israeli control over the West Bank. In his view, the Palestinian state, if there was to be one, should be east of the Jordan River, in Jordan—and the Hashemite monarchy that ruled Israel's neighbor to the east should come to an end. Naturally, after decades of secret but effective cooperation with Israeli Labor governments, Jordan found this shift of view in Israel's new government deeply alarming. Thus, while the Camp David Accords had tried to establish a plan for Palestinian "autonomy" in the West Bank, the Likud leadership in Israel never really supported that goal. And the PLO did not accept it either.

To solidify Israel's control over the West Bank, Israel's new government took a completely different approach to settlement policy. Instead of locating settlements near the Green Line and in the Jordan Valley for security purposes, the Likud government deliberately established settlements near large Arab population centers. It spent enormous sums of money building settlements and subsidizing Israelis to live in them. It appropriated more land, built more roads that divided Arab-populated regions, and enforced zoning and other ordinances that made it hard for Arabs to build homes in certain areas. Some of the most radical members of the Likud even favored "transferring" Arabs out of the West Bank (and Gaza) to speed the day when the majority population there would be Jewish. Also, many of the settlers who went to the new settlements near Arab-populated areas were nationalists, not people looking for cheap housing. Clearly, the Begin government, and that of Yitzhak Shamir after him, sought to create new "facts on the ground," demographic and otherwise, in the West Bank that would make a land-for-peace trade impossible. They succeeded fairly well in creating such facts: by 2003 the West Bank held 231 Jewish settlements and other civilian land use areas, containing about 182,000 settlers.

THE LEBANON MORASS

Having been chased out of Jordan in 1970–71, after Black September, the PLO leadership and its guerrilla fighters, known as *fedayeen*, migrated to Lebanon. In that country to Israel's north, Arafat's organization found friendly ground. Some 250,000 Palestinian refugees were living in Lebanon, many in squalid camps, and they were not allowed to become Lebanese citizens. In 1975 the PLO helped foment a civil war in Lebanon. The fighting and the political chaos that ensued enabled Arafat's organization to establish another state-within-a-state, in southern Lebanon. From there the fedayeen launched attacks against northern Israel.

In 1978, after cross-border raids had become a serious security problem, Israel sent its army into Lebanon to suppress the fedayeen. The incursion met with little longer-term success, however, and the problem only got worse.

In 1982 Defense Minister Ariel Sharon convinced the Israeli government to launch a large-scale invasion of Lebanon. The

Remains of a school bus destroyed by terrorists on the border between Israel and Lebanon. Eight children were killed and 20 others injured. After the PLO was forced out of Jordan in 1970–71, it moved to southern Lebanon, where it continued to carry out terrorist attacks against Israel, ultimately prompting Israel's invasion of Lebanon in 1982.

campaign, Sharon argued, would destroy the PLO, thus solving the security problem along Israel's northern border, facilitating further Israeli settlement of the West Bank, and ultimately setting the stage for the "Palestinianization" of Jordan. The Lebanon invasion would also chip away at Syrian influence in Lebanon; Syria, which had intervened in the Lebanese civil war, controlled what was left of Lebanon's government.

By summer, after about four months of fighting, Israeli forces reached Beirut, Lebanon's capital. There Arafat and his fedayeen were trapped. Before Israel could annihilate the PLO, however, the United States demanded that the Israelis end their campaign. Israel reluctantly complied, and Arafat and his men were allowed to evacuate the city. Arafat then established his new headquarters in Tunisia.

Getting out of Lebanon turned out to be hard for the Israeli military. Indeed, Israel occupied parts of Lebanon for the next 18 years. Gradually, the Israeli forces pulled back to a self-declared buffer area in southern Lebanon, hoping to keep the civilian population of northern Israel safe by so doing. But over time, Shi'a Muslims in southern Lebanon—who had initially welcomed Israeli soldiers for liberating their villages from the depredations of Arafat's Palestinian militias—turned against Israel. An organization called Hizballah, which was partly inspired by the 1979 Iranian revolution, arose and used terrorist methods and guerrilla war to force Israel to withdraw from Lebanon altogether. This Israel finally did in May 2000. By that time hundreds of Israeli soldiers had been killed, joining the more than 650 who had died in 1982 during the initial invasion.

The invasion and occupation of Lebanon proved costly to Israel (and to the Likud government in particular) in other respects. It prompted a rift with the United States and seriously divided public opinion within Israel. It also led to international condemnation, particularly for the notorious September 1982 massacres at the Sabra and Shatila refugee camps. Those massacres, which claimed the lives of some 800 Palestinian civilians, were carried out by Lebanese militiamen allied with Israel after Israeli forces had sealed off the camps. An Israeli commission later found Ariel Sharon indirectly responsible, prompting his resignation.

As the Israeli military got bogged down in southern Lebanon and Yasir Arafat settled into his new headquarters in Tunis, Tunisia, Israel's Likud government struggled to pursue its domestic agenda. The 1982 invasion may have chased the PLO from Lebanon, as intended, but in a surprising way it complicated Likud's plans for the West Bank: the damage suffered by Arafat's PLO encouraged moderate Palestinians to contemplate negotiating with Israel over a possible two-state solution in which Israel's right to exist would be acknowledged and accepted—which was not what Likud wanted.

The attitude of Likud governments toward the West Bank generated much dissonance not only with the United States, but also within Israel. Likud and Labor views of the future of the occupied territories and of Israel's own political culture became increasingly polarized, the arguments increasingly bitter. Israel became a more divided polity, not so much or mainly between Ashkenazim and Sephardim as between secular and religious, nationalist and more internationalist, socialist and non-socialist. A society that always had its rough edges, for having been under siege, became in some ways even rougher.

ECONOMIC STRIDES

The Likud, meanwhile, did not manage the Israeli economy notably better than had Labor. In the aftermath of the war in Lebanon, an inflationary spiral seized the economy and stifled economic growth. Many talented people left the country; the economy could not absorb the high-quality products of Israel's own universities. The economic troubles of the 1980s, however, finally convinced not only the Likud but also most of the Labor Party elite that serious economic reform was necessary. Starting with a national unity government that included both Labor and Likud in 1984, Israel reined in inflation and began to privatize many government-owned industries and, in other ways, to liberalize the economy.

The result was that, between 1991 and 1996, the Israeli economy grew faster than any other industrial economy, averaging 5.2 percent per year. By the early 1990s the Israeli economy was larger than that of all its immediate neighbors combined (Egypt, Jordan, Syria, Lebanon, and the Palestinian areas), even though

Israel had just a fraction of the population of those neighbors. Israel was no longer considered a developing economy, as its gross domestic product per capita exceeded that of some members of the European Union.

During this time, too, Israel's economy changed. The country became less dependent on exporting citrus, flowers, and diamonds and developed into one of the high-technology centers of the world. Today, agriculture accounts for only 4 percent of Israel's GDP; manufacturing contributes 37 percent, and services 59 percent. Israel's location and its human talent positioned it very well for the advent of globalization and the Internet economy. Israel's own ability to produce technological innovations, from places like the Weizmann Institute of Science and the Technion University, came of age.

Those innovations included military equipment. Israel had

Chaim Weizmann lays the cornerstone for the Weizmann Institute of Science in Rehovot. Since the foundation of the State of Israel, the country has maintained a technological advantage over its Arab neighbors.

secretly produced a few nuclear weapons from its plant in Dimona by 1969, though Israel has never admitted to having nuclear weapons. Israel's nuclear science program was aided by France during the time the two countries were allies. In the 1980s and 1990s, Israel's scientists greatly refined Israel's nuclear arsenal, and its military technology in general. Although Israel remains dependent on the United States to deploy large weapons systems like fighter aircraft, it has become increasingly self-reliant in other areas. Israel produces first-rate military electronics, and has even launched its own surveillance satellite into orbit—quite a feat for such a small country.

Israel also benefited economically from the collapse of the Soviet Union and the end of communism. By the 1970s, pressure on the Soviet Union to allow freer emigration had begun to result in significant numbers of Jews leaving the country, and many of them went to live in Israel. But in the dying days of the Soviet empire, what had been a substantial number became a flood. Israel's population rose by more than 10 percent in just a few years as Russian-speaking Jews immigrated to Israel. Russian language signs popped up all over the country as the Israeli system struggled to integrate and absorb nearly a million people—a very significant number for such a small country. The Russian émigrés were, by and large, a very well educated group. Israel's economic success in the late 1980s and 1990s owed much to their contributions.

LIKUD, LABOR, AND THE WEST BANK

The Likud ascendancy that began in May 1977 did not last unbroken for very long. Some elections in the 1980s were so close that Labor and Likud ruled together. A trend toward smaller parties doing better and winning more seats also arose. In the 1950s, 1960s, and 1970s, Labor and Likud between them averaged about 90 out of 120 Knesset seats. Before the elections of January 2003, between them the two parties held only 57 seats. In the January 2003 election, they got 57 seats between the two of them. The religious parties, and in particular a Sephardic political party called Shas, grew, as did more extreme right- and left-wing parties like Moledet and Meretz. This has made coalition building and maintenance more difficult, and it has made governments less stable.

The Labor Party's biggest comeback began in 1992, when Yitzhak Rabin won the prime ministry for the second time. Rabin led the country until his assassination, by an Israeli law student opposed to the peace process with the Palestinians, in 1995. Fellow Labor Party member Shimon Peres succeeded Rabin and served until the 1996 election, which the Likud won, making Binyamin Netanyahu the prime minister. Labor again won in the 1999 election, and Ehud Barak became prime minister. But Barak lost to Likud and Ariel Sharon in February 2001. In short, neither party is dominant today; the two main parties seem to take turns in office. Why this is so has mainly to do with foreign policy and security issues, and here we must again return to Israel's relationship with the Palestinians.

After the Gulf War of 1991—during which a broad-based international coalition led by the United States expelled Iraq from Kuwait, which Iraq had invaded the previous year—U.S. officials tried to take advantage of the moment to drive the Arab-Israeli peace process forward. The United States managed to convene a major conference in Madrid, Spain, that for the first time brought Israel and all its neighbors together, face-to-face, at the same negotiating table. It was a major psychological breakthrough. Unfortunately, not much tangible progress was made at or after Madrid, particularly on the Palestinian track. Israel's Likud prime minister, Yitzhak Shamir, refused to negotiate with Arafat and the PLO, and no other credible Palestinian interlocutor could be found.

When Rabin became prime minister in 1992, he vowed to make

Bill Clinton watches as Yitzhak Rabin shakes hands with Yasir Arafat in the White House garden, September 13, 1993. The two leaders had signed a declaration of principles that provided conditions for the creation of an autonomous Palestinian state in the West Bank and Gaza Strip.

the peace process work. Rabin wanted to end Israel's occupation of the West Bank, or at least most of it, for several reasons. First of all, since 1988 the Palestinians had been in open, violent revolt against Israeli rule in the West Bank and Gaza. This revolt, which Palestinians referred to as the *intifada*, or "shaking off," had claimed scores of lives. Second, Rabin believed, as did most Labor Party supporters, that it was morally wrong for Israel to rule a people against their will, and that the occupation was corroding Israeli society and its values. A third consideration was that radical Islamist Palestinians were gaining strength, and these radicals, typified by an organization called Hamas, were spreading terrorism throughout Israel.

So Rabin made the decision to negotiate secretly with the PLO.

After talks held in Oslo, Norway, Israel and the PLO officially recognized each other. On September 13, 1993, Rabin and Arafat signed a declaration of principles at a ceremony on the White House lawn.

The Oslo accords called for a two-phase process. In the first phase, which was to last five years, the Palestinian Authority would take over the governing of some areas in the West Bank and Gaza as Israel withdrew. The two parties would cooperate on security and other issues. At the end of the five-year interim period, Israel and the Palestinian Authority, having established mutual confidence and trust, would enter into negotiations to resolve the outstanding issues: the nature of the Palestinian state, final borders, the status of Jerusalem, the claims of Palestinian refugees, the fate of Jewish settlements.

IMPLEMENTATION OF THE OSLO ACCORDS

It was not easy to move from a declaration of principles to a working negotiation designed to bring about peace, however. Some Israelis continued to distrust Arafat and the PLO and were strongly opposed to the Oslo accords. Rabin knew he was taking a risk to trust Arafat and the PLO, but he believed that the status quo was unacceptable—and that the situation was bound to get worse. Divisions in Israel over the government's strategy were bitter, and these divisions were mirrored among Jews in the United States and elsewhere concerned about Israel's security and future.

In 1994 Arafat and his associates returned from exile to the Palestinian territories, where they began to rule areas that Israel had vacated. These areas included most of Gaza and parts of the West Bank. By the end of 1995, Israel had withdrawn its military government and the Palestinian Authority was in control of 95 percent of all Palestinians in the West Bank and Gaza. Israel, however, maintained overall security control. Extensive and detailed agreements were worked out covering economic issues, Palestinian police and security forces, and dozens of other subjects. The hope was that practical cooperation would lay a basis for trust and that with trust the two sides could negotiate a final end to the conflict.

The Oslo accords paved the way for better Israeli relations with some Arab states and other countries previously hostile to the Jewish state. Israel and Jordan signed a peace treaty in October 1994. Informal relations between Israel and Qatar, Morocco, Tunisia, and several other Arab states also advanced. The Arab economic boycott of Israel was ended formally, and Israel was able to trade with many countries that had before shunned it. Israel was also able to establish diplomatic relations and open trade relations with major countries such as India and China. Israel thus benefited from the Oslo process in many ways.

But it did not benefit in the main way Israelis had hoped. A renewed effort to make peace with Syria failed when Syria refused to consider any compromises. Worse, anti-Israel terrorism from the Palestinian territories increased, prompting Israel to slow down its withdrawal from the occupied territories. Meanwhile, Jewish settlements in the West Bank and Gaza mushroomed. By the mid-1990s, more than 140,000 Jewish settlers lived in the territories—a source of considerable resentment among Palestinians.

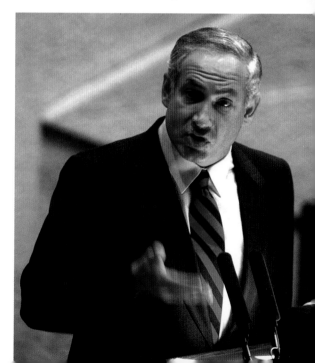

Binyamin Netanyahu was elected prime minister in 1996 because many Israelis did not trust Yasir Arafat to negotiate in good faith.

Instead of building trust, the implementation of the Oslo accords eroded it. Israelis wanted a tougher approach to Arafat, and that is why in 1996 they elected Likud's hard-line Binyamin Netanyahu.

From the signing of the Oslo accords in 1993 until a major summit at Camp David in the summer of 2000, most Israelis (and some others) were uncertain about whether Arafat was really a reliable partner for peace. Some believed that the PLO leader was behind the terrorism and that he never really intended to sign an end-of-conflict agreement. The most skeptical maintained that Arafat was merely trying to weaken Israel with the ultimate goal of destroying it. Others asserted that Arafat was allowing violence in order to get a better deal from Israel, for violent pressure was the Palestinians' only way to reduce Israeli demands. Still others believed that Arafat opposed the violence but was too weak to stop it, fearing that he might ignite a civil war among Palestinians.

THE SECOND *INTIFADA*

At the Camp David summit in the summer of 2000, Prime Minister Ehud Barak put before Arafat the most generous peace proposal any Israeli government had ever developed. It even included a willingness to turn over part of the Old City of Jerusalem to the Palestinians. Not only did Arafat not accept the offer, he refused even to negotiate seriously over it, or to make any counter-proposals. Then, in September 2000, most Israeli analysts believe that Arafat either ordered or abetted a small terror war started against Israel; it came to be called the second or Al-Aqsa *intifada*. The primary weapon in this *intifada* soon became the suicide bomber: a typically young Palestinian who would strap explosives to his or her body, go to a public place where large numbers of Israelis congregated, and detonate the bomb. Many Israelis suspected this terror campaign of being directed by top Palestinian leaders, if not by Arafat himself. Later, when Arafat's signature on documents directing payments to the families of suicide bombers was found, these suspicions were confirmed.

Despite the violence, the Barak government tried again to negotiate with Arafat, putting forward an even more generous peace proposal during talks held at the Egyptian resort town of Taba in January 2001. But the Palestinians continued to balk.

The failure of the peace talks to produce a settlement spelled the end of Ehud Barak's government. The Israeli people, angered and weary after all the violence, and disillusioned with the peace process, rejected Barak and elected Likud's Ariel Sharon as prime minister in February 2001—an event that most people had thought impossible only a few months before.

Sharon ruled at the head of a national unity government, with significant Labor Party participation, but he took what most observers considered a hard-line approach to Palestinians and the occupied territories. Palestinian terrorist attacks were met with the imposition of strict military curfews in Palestinian towns, with the destruction of the homes of terrorists' families, and, later, with what Israel called "targeted killings" (assassinations of Palestinian leaders Israel deemed responsible for terrorism).

Israeli and U.S. officials repeatedly called on Arafat to condemn the violence. While he did publicly disavow attacks on Israeli citizens—responsibility for which was frequently claimed by terrorist groups such as Hamas—many observers questioned Arafat's sincerity. For one thing, a group that carried out many of the suicide bombings, the Al-Aqsa Martyrs Brigade, had links to Arafat's Fatah faction. And in early 2002, Israeli forces intercepted a 50-ton shipment of arms and explosives from Iran that was destined for the Palestinian Authority. It was just a few months later that the Israelis uncovered the documents indicating that Arafat was paying the families of suicide bombers.

Amid a rash of deadly suicide bombings coinciding with the

Ariel Sharon waves during a victory celebration on January 29, 2003, at Tel Aviv Fairgrounds. Israeli voters kept Sharon's Likud Party in power in the Knesset, after which Sharon promised to build a new "unity" government to combat Israel's internal and external problems.

beginning of the Jewish holiday of Passover in March 2002, Sharon's government mounted a siege of the Palestinian Authority's compound. Israeli tanks and bulldozers destroyed many of the buildings and trapped Arafat and his top aides inside his head-quarters for more than a month before withdrawing. Following more suicide bombings in September, Israel once again laid siege to Arafat's compound, demolishing all but one building.

While the violence had subsided somewhat by year's end, peri-odic Palestinian terrorist attacks and Israeli retaliation continued, and no one precluded the possibility of another major outbreak. By the beginning of 2003, the second *intifada* had claimed the lives of more than 2,000 Palestinians and more than 700 Israelis.

THE 2003 ELECTIONS

In early November 2002 Ariel Sharon's national unity coalition government collapsed after the Labor Party refused to support the budget. The dispute involved a perennial source of contention within Israeli society: Jewish settlements in the occupied territories. Labor wanted funds earmarked for support of the settlements to be allocated instead for social programs within Israel proper. Jewish society remains divided by the issue of the settlements. Some see them as an impediment to peace with the Palestinians; others believe they not only enhance the security of all Israel but also represent the fulfillment of the Jewish people's resettlement of their ancestral lands. By the end of 2002, some 225,000 Jewish settlers lived in about 150 settlements in the West Bank and Gaza.

Elections held in January 2003 offered Israelis clear choices regarding settlement policy and the larger issue of how to deal with the Palestinians. Sharon, the Likud's pro-settlement leader, advocated an uncompromising stance: he had consistently demanded the cessation of all terrorist violence against Israelis as a precondition to negotiations with the Palestinians, and he publicly dismissed the possibility of negotiations while Yasir Arafat remained the Palestinians' leader. (A similar position was enunciated by the U.S. administration of President George W. Bush. On June 24, 2002, Bush stated that he supported an independent Palestinian state and the end of Israeli occupation of most of the West Bank, but only if the Palestinians would end their terrorism and develop new political leadership that could be trusted to negotiate in good faith.)

Sharon's Labor Party opponent, Amram Mitzna, promised to evacuate Jewish settlements in the West Bank and Gaza within a year if elected. Mitzna, who had commanded Israeli forces in the West Bank during the first *intifada*, declared that a military solution to the Palestinian uprising would never succeed. He advocated reopening peace negotiations with the Palestinians even if terrorist attacks continued because otherwise a few Palestinian extremists would be able to dictate Israel's agenda.

When Israelis went to the polls in late January, they seemed to endorse Sharon's more hawkish approach to the Palestinians. Likud won a resounding victory, capturing 38 seats in the Knesset and guaranteeing Sharon another term as prime minister. Labor suffered its worst electoral showing ever, winning just 19 seats. Although Sharon expressed his desire to organize another national unity government, Amram Mitzna declared that Labor would not participate, which meant that Sharon's governing coalition might have to include political parties from the far right. It remained to be seen if Mitzna would change his mind, or if the Labor Party would replace him with another leader.

If Israelis by 2003 were divided over policy and leadership questions, so too were Palestinians. Many Palestinians had grown disillusioned with Arafat's leadership; his Palestinian Authority administration was notoriously corrupt and widely regarded as inept. In addition, some Palestinians had begun to question the wisdom of the Al-Aqsa *intifada*, which, despite the loss of so many lives, had apparently not brought the Palestinians any closer to an independent state of their own. Of course, gauging public opinion among Palestinians is difficult because the Palestinian Authority is not a democratic organization and does not tolerate a free press.

Many people, particularly in the Arab world and in some European countries, believe that Israel is responsible for the violence directed against it, because it will not withdraw from the West Bank, Gaza, and East Jerusalem and allow a fully independent Palestinian state to come into being. Some also accuse Israel of deliberately targeting Palestinian civilians—for more Palestinians have been killed in the Al-Aqsa *intifada* than Jews. Many think that Yasir Arafat would accept a final, two-state solution if he got the terms he seeks for a Palestinian state.

Judging from the outcome of the January 2003 election, most Israelis reject this view. As they see things, Israeli governments led by both Labor and Likud have expressed their willingness to allow a Palestinian state to come into being. Most Israelis believe, too, that most civilian casualties among the Palestinians have been caused by mistakes and by Palestinian terrorists' use of civilians as human shields. As most Israelis see it, Israeli forces do not deliberately target civilians, while Palestinian terrorists nearly always do, and therefore they find it hard to understand how outsiders can equate Israeli and Palestinian casualties. As a result of this, some Israelis believe that much opposition to Israeli policies is anti-Semitic in nature, not just anti-Israel at heart. If one remembers the reasons for Zionism in the first place and the psychological impact of the Holocaust on modern Jewish history, it is easy to see why some people take this view.

Whether these views are right or wrong—and whether many Palestinian views are right or wrong—is almost beside the point. The fact is that very negative views of the other exist on both sides, and as a result many observers are pessimistic that the two sides can be reconciled anytime soon. These observers foresee a test of wills: with Israel refusing to allow Palestinian violence to gain them political advantages, and Palestinians refusing to allow Israel to be secure until its leaders give them what they want. Others are more optimistic, believing that both leaderships—probably after Arafat and Sharon—will come to realize that military solutions are impossible, and will find a way to compromise. Only time will tell who is right.

"The land of Israel was the birthplace of the Jewish people," reads the 1948 Israeli declaration of independence. "Here their spiritual, religious and national identity was formed. Here they achieved independence and created a culture of national and universal significance. Here they wrote and gave the Bible to the world."

Looking Forward

In May 2003, Israel celebrated its 55th year of independence. Israel is a young country with an old civilization and a very long history. No one can predict the future, but it seems clear that achieving peace with its neighbors would greatly enhance Israel's prospects.

Even if peace is not achieved, however, Israel can survive and prosper. It is not a post-Holocaust "colonial implantation" as its adversaries claim, but a people rooted to their land and culture. Israel has talented people, a strong military and economy, and important friends and supporters around the world, including the government of the United States.

A FLOURISHING CULTURE

Israel has succeeded in creating a modern Jewish civilization that is the center of world Jewish history and culture. Outside of Israel, Jews constitute a minority that ranges from

The blue stripes on Israel's flag were inspired by the Hebrew *tallit* (prayer shawl); the Star of David, a symbol of the Jewish people, dates to biblical times.

small (an estimated 2 percent in the United States, for example) to minuscule (of the world's more than 6 billion people, only about 13.5 million are Jewish). Even in the Middle East, Jews make up a small percentage of the population: they are outnumbered by some 20 to 1 considering only the countries that share a border with Israel—Egypt, Lebanon, Syria, Jordan, and the territories of the Palestinian Authority. But of the approximately 6 million people living in Israel today, more than 80 percent are Jews. Although there were still more Jews living in the United States than in Israel in 2003, with higher intermarriage and assimilation rates for American Jews, and with Israel's continued population growth, those trend lines are expected to cross in just a few years.

In Israel modern Hebrew literature, theater, music, and the other arts—which blend Eastern and Western influences to produce a unique result—are thriving. At the same time, Israeli Arabs, both Christian and Muslim, also contribute much to the state and its culture—though there is mounting fear among Israeli Jews and Arabs alike that their communal relations are worsening, not getting better.

In contemporary Israel, tensions abound between the secular

and the religious, and between left-wing and right-wing political views. But in many respects, diversity and differences of opinion are the hallmark of any open society, and Israel's democracy remains strong.

THE PROSPECT FOR PEACE

If peace between Israel and its neighbors, especially the Palestinians, can be achieved, the result might well be a flourishing not just of the State of Israel, but of the entire Eastern Mediterranean region. It was the dream of Israel's Zionist founders to normalize Jewish history—that is, to resume the history of the Jewish people in their own homeland. In the Middle East, as ancient history reveals, what was normal was not always peaceful and prosperous; but Israel's hope is to be a secure and productive member of the community of nations while retaining its own unique heritage and culture.

Whether it will succeed in this depends a great deal on the outcome of the struggle going on in the Muslim world today, between the mainstream civilization of Islam and a small group of fundamentalist extremists. Even if Israel can make peace with the PLO, that peace could be overwhelmed by the victory of Islamic extremists in Israel's region. If those extremists get control of entire countries, and those countries have weapons of mass destruction, Israel's very existence could be imperiled. In a very real sense, Israel's future depends on America's victory in the war against Islamist terrorism. In that war, the United States has no more loyal ally than Israel.

CHRONOLOGY

4000 B.C.: Traditional beginning of the Jewish people with the patriarch Abraham.

Ca. 1220 B.C.: Moses leads Israelites out of Egypt.

Ca. 1180–1100 B.C.: Israelite conquest of Canaan under Joshua and the Prophets.

Ca. 1013 B.C.: David becomes king of Israel.

Ca. 1006 B.C.: David conquers Jerusalem from the Jebusites.

Ca. 973–933 B.C.: Reign of Solomon and the building of the First Temple.

Ca. 933 B.C.: The Israelite kingdom divides into Israel and Judea.

722 B.C.: Assyrian conquest of Israel; exile of the 10 tribes.

586 B.C.: Babylonian conquest of Judea, end of the First Commonwealth, and first exile.

Ca. 537 B.C.: Restoration under Cyrus the Great.

Ca. 517 B.C.: Second Temple and Second Commonwealth begin.

331 B.C.: Alexander the Great conquers Judea.

165 B.C.: Jewish rebellion against Assyrian Greeks; Temple is rededicated (Hanukkah).

63 B.C.: Romans conquer Judea.

A.D. 70: The Second Temple is destroyed.

135: Bar Kokhba Rebellion is crushed by Rome; second exile begins; Judea is renamed Palestine.

634: Arab Muslims conquer Palestine.

1099: Crusader Kingdom is established in Palestine.

1187: Battle of Hittin; Saladin destroys Crusader Kingdom.

1492: Jews are expelled from Spain.

1517: Palestine comes under Ottoman rule.

1897: First Zionist Congress at Basel, Switzerland.

1917: The Balfour Declaration commits Britain to facilitate the creation of a homeland for Jews in Palestine.

1920: Establishment of the Palestine Mandate; founding of the Histadrut, Haganah, and Hebrew University.

CHRONOLOGY

1933: First British edicts restricting Jewish immigration to Palestine are issued.

1939–45: World War II and the Holocaust.

1947: Partition Commission and Resolution.

1948: Proclamation of Israel's independence and the War of Independence.

1949: Armistices are signed with the Arab nations; the first Knesset election is held.

1956: The Sinai Campaign.

1967: Six-Day (or June) War.

1973: October War.

1977: Egyptian president Anwar Sadat visits Israel and addresses the Knesset.

1978: Camp David summit.

1979: Israel-Egyptian peace treaty is ratified.

1982: Israel invades Lebanon.

1988–91: First *intifada*, or Palestinian uprising, takes place.

1993: Oslo accords are signed in Washington.

1994: Israel-Jordan peace treaty is signed.

1995: In November, Prime Minister Yitzhak Rabin is assassinated.

2000: In May the second Camp David summit fails; in September the second, or Al-Aqsa, *intifada* begins.

2001: In February, the Taba summit fails; in March, Ariel Sharon becomes prime minister of Israel.

2003: Sharon's Likud Party wins resounding victory in January 28 elections; Labor Party suffers its worst electoral performance ever.

GLOSSARY

annex—to incorporate new territory (as territory seized in war) into a country.

anti-Semitism—hostility toward or discrimination against Jews as a group.

aquifer—an underground source of freshwater.

Ashkenazim—Jews of European cultural origin.

Cold War—a worldwide political and ideological conflict between the Soviet Union and the United States in the period between the late 1940s and the early 1990s.

Eretz Yisrael—literally, "the Land of Israel," this term refers to the Promised Land that the Jewish people believe was given to them by God.

gross domestic product—the total value of goods and services produced in a country in a one-year period.

Haganah—a Jewish defense force of British Mandate times, which was the forerunner of the Israeli army.

halacha—Jewish religious law.

haredim—ultra-Orthodox Jews who typically do not accept the legitimacy of the State of Israel but who reside in the country for religious reasons.

Histadrut—a labor-union federation formed during the British Mandate era.

Irgun—a Revisionist paramilitary movement of Mandate times.

kibbutz—a collective agricultural settlement.

Knesset—Israel's 120-seat parliament.

Mandate—authorization given by the League of Nations to a member country (for example, France or Great Britain) to administer a territory (such as parts of the Middle East) after World War I.

Mizrahi—a religious Zionist movement.

nationalize—to place a privately owned company, commercial operation, or industry under government control.

GLOSSARY

Palmach—an elite special-forces unit within the Haganah.

Sephardim—Jews of non-Western origin.

Tzahal—an acronym for the Israeli military.

Yishuv—the Zionist resettlement community during Mandate times.

Zionism—the modern national movement of the Jewish people.

FURTHER READING

GENERAL TEXTS

Garfinkle, Adam. *Politics and Society in Modern Israel*. Armonk, N.Y.: M. E. Sharpe, 2000.

Peretz, Don. *The Government and Politics of Israel*. Boulder, Colo.: Westview, 1983.

Reich, Bernard. *Israel: Land of Tradition and Conflict*. Boulder, Colo.: Westview, 1985.

JEWISH HISTORY

Grayzel, Solomon. *A History of the Jews*. Philadelphia: Jewish Publication Society, 1968.

Margolis, Max L., and Alexander Marx. *A History of the Jewish People*. New York: Meridian Books, 1958.

MODERN HISTORY

O'Brien, Conor Cruise. *The Siege: The Saga of Israel and Zionism*. New York: Simon & Schuster, 1986.

Sacher, Howard M. *A History of Israel from the Rise of Zionism to Our Time*. New York: Knopf, 1976.

Sykes, Christopher. *Crossroads to Israel*. New York: World, 1966.

ZIONISM

Avineri, Shlomo. *The Making of Modern Zionism*. New York: Basic Books, 1981.

Laqueur, Walter. *A History of Zionism*. New York: Holt, Rinehart & Winston, 1972.

POLITICAL CULTURE

Aronoff, Myron. *Israeli Visions and Divisions*. New Brunswick, N.J.: Transaction, 1989.

Eisenstadt, S. N. *Israeli Society*. New York: Basic Books, 1967.

Goldscheider, Calvin. *Israel's Changing Society*. Boulder, Colo.: Westview, 1996.

Wistrich, Robert, ed. *The Shaping of Israeli Identity*. London: Frank Cass, 1995.

FURTHER READING

ARAB-ISRAELI CONFLICT

Kemp, Geoffrey, and Jeremy Pressman. *Point of No Return*. Washington, D.C.: Carnegie Endowment, 1997.

Laqueur, Walter, and Barry Rubin. *The Arab-Israeli Reader*. New York: Penguin, 2001.

Ovendale, Ritchie. *The Origins of the Arab-Israeli Wars*. New York: Longman, 1984.

Quandt, William. *Decade of Decisions*. Berkeley: University of California Press, 1994.

Rubinstein, Alvin Z., ed. *The Arab-Israeli Conflict*. New York: HarperCollins, 1990.

Safran, Nadav. *Israel: The Embattled Ally*. Cambridge, Mass.: Harvard University Press, 1981.

Sicherman, Harvey. *Palestinian Autonomy*. Boulder, Colo.: Westview, 1992.

BIOGRAPHY AND AUTOBIOGRAPHY

Begin, Menachem. *The Revolt*. New York: Nash, 1981.

Ben-Gurion, David. *Israel: A Personal History*. New York: Funk & Wagnalls, 1971.

Dayan, Moshe. *The Story of My Life*. New York: Morrow, 1976.

Elon, Amos. *Herzl*. New York: Holt, Rinehart & Winston, 1975.

Meir, Golda. *My Life*. New York: Putnam, 1975.

Rabin, Yitzhak. *The Rabin Memoirs*. Boston: Little, Brown, 1975.

Reinharz, Judah. *Chaim Weizmann: The Making of a Zionist Leader*. New York: Oxford University Press, 1985.

Sharon, Ariel. *Warrior*. New York: Simon & Schuster, 1989.

Weizmann, Chaim. *Trial and Error*. Philadelphia: Jewish Publication Society, 1949.

INTERNET RESOURCES

http://www.cia.gov/cia/publications/factbook/geos/is.html

The Central Intelligence Agency's Israel site contains statistical and background information.

http://memory.loc.gov/frd/cs/iltoc.html

The Library of Congress country study provides in-depth information about Israel's geography, history, economy, society, and foreign policy, among other topics.

http://www.haaretzdaily.com

The online version of one of Israel's leading newspapers, *Ha'aretz*, provides news and feature articles.

http://www.mfa.gov.il/mfa/home.asp

The website of Israel's Ministry of Foreign Affairs contains a variety of links to news stories and Israeli perspectives on diplomatic issues.

http://www.goisrael.com

Website of Israel's Ministry of Tourism.

INDEX

Numbers in **bold italic** refer to captions.

INDEX

PICTURE CREDITS

Cover photos: (front) (all images) IMS Communications; (back) IMS Communications

CONTRIBUTORS

The **FOREIGN POLICY RESEARCH INSTITUTE (FPRI)** served as editorial consultants for the MODERN MIDDLE EAST NATIONS series. FPRI is one of the nation's oldest "think tanks." The Institute's Middle East Program focuses on Gulf security, monitors the Arab-Israeli peace process, and sponsors an annual conference for teachers on the Middle East, plus periodic briefings on key developments in the region.

Among the FPRI's trustees is a former Secretary of State and a former Secretary of the Navy (and among the FPRI's former trustees and interns, two current Undersecretaries of Defense), not to mention two university presidents emeritus, a foundation president, and several active or retired corporate CEOs.

The scholars of FPRI include a former aide to three U.S. Secretaries of State, a Pulitzer Prize–winning historian, a former president of Swarthmore College and a Bancroft Prize–winning historian, and two former staff members of the National Security Council. And the FPRI counts among its extended network of scholars—especially its Inter-University Study Groups—representatives of diverse disciplines, including political science, history, economics, law, management, religion, sociology, and psychology.

DR. HARVEY SICHERMAN is president and director of the Foreign Policy Research Institute in Philadelphia, Pennsylvania. He has extensive experience in writing, research, and analysis of U.S. foreign and national security policy, both in government and out. He served as Special Assistant to Secretary of State Alexander M. Haig Jr. and as a member of the Policy Planning Staff of Secretary of State James A. Baker III. Dr. Sicherman was also a consultant to Secretary of the Navy John F. Lehman Jr. (1982–1987) and Secretary of State George Shultz (1988).

A graduate of the University of Scranton (B.S., History, 1966), Dr. Sicherman earned his Ph.D. at the University of Pennsylvania (Political Science, 1971), where he received a Salvatori Fellowship. He is author or editor of numerous books and articles, including *America the Vulnerable: Our Military Problems and How to Fix Them* (FPRI, 2002) and *Palestinian Autonomy, Self-Government and Peace* (Westview Press, 1993). He edits *Peacefacts*, an FPRI bulletin that monitors the Arab-Israeli peace process.

ADAM GARFINKLE is editor of *The National Interest* magazine. He was a staff member of the U.S. Commission on National Security/21st Century and holds a Ph.D. in international relations from the University of Pennsylvania.